Post-Digital Letterpress Printing

This book presents an overview of the convergence of traditional letterpress with contemporary digital design and fabrication practices.

Reflecting on the role of letterpress within the emergent hybrid post-digital design process, contributors present historical and contemporary analysis, grounded in case studies and current practice. The main themes covered include the research on letterpress as a technology and medium; a reflection on the contribution of letterpress to arts and design education; and current artistic and communication design practice merging past, present, and future digital fabrication processes.

This will be of interest to scholars working in graphic design, communication design, book design, typography, typeface design, design history, printing, and production technologies.

Pedro Amado is Assistant Professor in the Faculty of Fine Arts at the University of Porto, Portugal, and a member of the i2ADS Research Institute, Porto.

Ana Catarina Silva is Assistant Professor in the School of Design at the Polytechnic Institute of Cávado and Ave, Portugal, and a member of the ID+/CAOS Research Institute, Barcelos.

Vítor Quelhas is Assistant Professor in the School of Media Arts and Design at the Polytechnic Institute of Porto, Portugal, and a member of the ID+, Aveiro, and Unimad Research Institute, Porto.

Routledge Focus on Art History and Visual Studies

Routledge Focus on Art History and Visual Studies presents short-form books on varied topics within the fields of art history and visual studies.

Post-Conflict Monuments in Bosnia and Herzegovina
Unfinished Histories
Uroš Čvoro

Robert Motherwell, Abstraction, and Philosophy
Robert Hobbs

Jimmie Durham, Europe, and the Art of Relations
Andrea Feeser

World-Forming and Contemporary Art
Jessica Holtaway

The Power and Fluidity of Girlhood in Henry Darger's Art
Leisa Rundquist

Buckminster Fuller's World Game and Its Legacy
Timothy Stott

Post-Digital Letterpress Printing
Research, Education and Practice
Edited by Pedro Amado, Ana Catarina Silva and Vítor Quelhas

For more information about this series, please visit: https://www.routledge.com/Routledge-Focus-on-Art-History-and-Visual-Studies/book-series/FOCUSAH

Post-Digital Letterpress Printing
Research, Education and Practice

**Edited by Pedro Amado,
Ana Catarina Silva and
Vítor Quelhas**

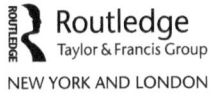

NEW YORK AND LONDON

First published 2022
by Routledge
605 Third Avenue, New York, NY 10158

and by Routledge
2 Park Square, Milton Park, Abingdon, Oxon, OX14 4RN

Routledge is an imprint of the Taylor & Francis Group, an informa business

© 2022 selection and editorial matter, Pedro Amado, Ana Catarina Silva and Vítor Quelhas; individual chapters, the contributors

The right of Pedro Amado, Ana Catarina Silva and Vítor Quelhas to be identified as the authors of the editorial material, and of the authors for their individual chapters, has been asserted in accordance with sections 77 and 78 of the Copyright, Designs and Patents Act 1988.

All rights reserved. No part of this book may be reprinted or reproduced or utilised in any form or by any electronic, mechanical, or other means, now known or hereafter invented, including photocopying and recording, or in any information storage or retrieval system, without permission in writing from the publishers.

Trademark notice: Product or corporate names may be trademarks or registered trademarks, and are used only for identification and explanation without intent to infringe.

Library of Congress Cataloging-in-Publication Data
A catalog record for this title has been requested

ISBN: 978-1-032-00180-7 (hbk)
ISBN: 978-1-032-00184-5 (pbk)
ISBN: 978-1-003-17311-3 (ebk)

DOI: 10.4324/9781003173113

Typeset in Times New Roman
by Deanta Global Publishing Services, Chennai, India

Contents

List of Figures vii
Contributors ix
Acknowledgements xvii
Foreword: Johanna Drucker xviii
Introduction xxi

PART I
Introduction: Research 1

Part Research Highlight: The Seven Lives of a Typeface: Material and Immaterial Convergences 3
AMELIA HUGILL-FONTANEL

1 **Appropriating Printing** 9
 CAROLINE ARCHER-PARRÉ

2 **Orlando Erasto Portela: Relations Between the Creative Process and Letterpress Printing Methods of an (Almost) Unknown Designer from the Mid-Twentieth Century** 19
 NUNO COELHO

3 *The Mark on the Wall* 30
 ANE THON KNUTSEN

PART II
Introduction: Education 39

Part Education Highlight: Poiesis and Purpose: Lessons in Making 41
CATHERINE DIXON

Contents

4 The Role of the Letterpress Workshop   47
RÚBEN DIAS AND SOFIA MEIRA

5 From Letterpress to Screen: Learning from a Modular Type System   56
ROBERTO GAMONAL ARROYO AND ANDREU BALIUS PLANELLES

6 PDLPX: The Post-Digital Letterpress Print Exchange: Methodological Innovation in the Exploration of Contemporary Letterpress Practice   65
CHRIS WILSON

7 Letterpress Experiments in a Design Course   75
RITA CARVALHO

PART III
Introduction: Practice   85

Part Practice Highlight: The Rising Letters – Seven Criteria for the Typographic Design of a Letterpress Archive: Proposing a dual, visual and sound analysis, in the extensive survey and registration of the movable type characters in two countries (observed and considered after twenty-five years have passed)   87
JORGE DOS REIS

8 Digital Fabrication: Expanding Access to and Preservation of Letterpress Printing   95
ERIN BECKLOFF

9 Resisting Hyper-Digitalisation: Investigating Hybrid Practices in Contemporary Graphic Design   104
LUCREZIA RUSSO

10 Computational Design Letterpress: From Procedural Programming to Modular Printing   113
PEDRO AMADO AND ANA CATARINA SILVA

Conclusion   123
PEDRO AMADO, ANA CATARINA SILVA AND VÍTOR QUELHAS

Index   125

Figures

P1.1 Letterpress Type. From Right Column, Top to Bottom: Goudy Cloister Initials Relief Type in Photopolymer; Photo-Etched Magnesium; Modern Lead-Alloy Cast from Original Brass Matrices; Laser-Engraved Maple Wood; Stereolithographic Plastic; Fused Deposition Model 3D Print. Photograph by Jiageng Lin   5

2.1 Three Labels of Soaps for the Brand Académico, Featuring an Illustration of a Male Student from the University of Coimbra Singing to Fado While Playing a Portuguese Guitar; Arraial, Featuring an Illustration of Two Men in a Folk Dress Playing Drums and Bagpipes; and Ceifeira, Featuring an Illustration of a Female Reaper Holding a Scythe, and a Wheat Branch   23

3.1 1837 Letterpress Prints on Newsprint That Make Up the Entire Short Story *The Mark on the Wall*, Written and Printed by Virginia Woolf. Kunstnernes Hus   36

P2.1 Retired Printer José Carlos Gianotti on Hand to Guide Students in Use of One of Their Two Vandercook Proofing Presses   44

5.1 Promotional Sheet of Super Tipo Veloz Showing its Many Combination Possibilities (Between 1942 and 1945 Approximately)   57

6.1 The 12 Prints Submitted to the Exchange   69

7.1 Praxe: It's Your Choice. Campo Grande Garden, Oct. 2009. BA Students (Design); José Sebastião (Photo)   80

P3.1 Typographic Thoughts. Cover Page of the Norwich Archive, 1996   88

8.1	Provisional Press Designed by Steve Garst with Wood Type Created by Scott Moore of Moore Wood Type and Posters by Brad Vetter	102
9.1	Mobile Uno: 3D Model (Top Left), Printing Test Results (Top Right), and Physical Prototype (Bottom)	110
10.1	Participants Inking a Collaborative Mixed-Media Imposition on a Flatbed Proof Press, while Others are 3D Printing a Module	118

Contributors

Pedro Amado
Assistant Professor, Faculty of Fine Arts, University of Porto, i2ADS Research Institute, Porto, Portugal

Pedro Amado is an Assistant Professor, Department of Design, Faculty of Fine Arts, University of Porto, Portugal (since 2017). Subdirector of the Faculty (during 2018), Member of the Board of Direction and Integrated Researcher of the i2ADS Research Institute (since 2019). Editor of the i2ADS journal. Member of the Scientific board of the Master in Graphic Design and Editorial Projects at FBAUP, Porto, Portugal (since 2018).

Amado holds a Ph.D. in Sciences and Technologies of Communication from the University of Aveiro, Portugal (2014), an MFA in Multimedia (2007), and a degree in Communication Design from the Faculty of Fine Arts of the University of Porto, Portugal (2002). He is currently an Assistant Professor of Web Design (HTML, CSS & JS), Interaction (UCD), Creative Coding (Processing), Typography, and Typeface Design at FBAUP. He is an integrated member of the board of direction of the i2ADS Research Institute (responsible for the design and communication), an ID+ collaborator, a founding member of the ATIPO typography association, and country delegate for the ATypI international association. Passionate about digital tinkering, an amateur letterpress printer, and a digital photographer, he focuses his research and development activities on typography and editorial design, computational and post-digital design, as well as human-computer interaction.

Ana Catarina Silva
Assistant Professor, School of Design, Polytechnic Institute of Cávado and Ave (IPCA), Barcelos, Portugal

Ana Catarina Silva is a teacher, a researcher and holds a Ph.D. in Sciences and Technologies of Communication (University of Porto, Portugal), with a thesis that studied the design of the technical book in a hybrid editorial context. Her research projects address a variety of fields and their borders, from hybrid editions to independent publishing, typography, letterpress or illustration. Books (and its forms) are her passion, and she's been teaching Typography, Editorial and Design Project in undergraduate and graduate degrees in Graphic Design and Digital Design since 2007 at IPCA. She is also a research member of CAOS (Communication, Art, Object, and Synergies/ID+ (Research Institute for Design, Media, and Culture), Barcelos, Portugal, a founding member of the ATIPO typography association, and a member of the Design Obs, a Portuguese Design Observatory.

Vítor Quelhas
Assistant Professor, Polytechnic Institute of Porto, School of Media Arts and Design, Porto, Portugal and ID+ Research Institute for Design, Media and Culture, Aveiro, Portugal and uniMAD, Porto, Portugal

Vítor Quelhas holds a Ph.D. in Design (Typography and Type Design) from the University of Aveiro, Portugal, an MFA in Multimedia Arts, and a degree in Communication Design/Graphic Arts, both granted by the Fine Arts School of the University of Porto, Portugal. Currently, he is an Assistant Professor of Communication Design, in the Department of Design, School of Media Arts and Design, Porto Polytechnic Institute, Portugal, where he coordinates the MA in Design.

He is an integrated member of the ID+ and uniMAD research centers, country delegate of the ATypI–Association Typographique Internationale, and a founding member of the ATIPO and the Typography Meeting International conference. He has been promoting his work in several conferences, exhibitions and publications. Among other distinctions, his work was recognized with two Certificates of Typographic Excellence, awarded by the Type Directors Club of New York.

Johanna Drucker
Distinguished Professor, Information Studies Faculty, UCLA, USA

Johanna Drucker is the Inaugural Breslauer Professor of Bibliographical Studies in the Department of Information Studies at UCLA, USA. She is internationally known for her work in the history of graphic design, typography, experimental poetry, fine art, and digital humanities. In addition, she has a reputation as a book artist, and her limited edition works are in special collections and libraries worldwide. Her most recent titles include *SpecLab: Digital Aesthetics and Speculative Computing* (2009), and *Graphic Design History: A Critical Guide* (2008, 2nd edition late 2012). She is currently working on a database memoir, *ALL*, the online *Museum of Writing* in collaboration with University College London and King's College, and a letterpress project titled *Stochastic Poetics*. A collaboratively written work, *Digital_Humanities*, with Jeffrey Schnapp, Todd Presner, Peter Lunenfeld, and Anne Burdick is forthcoming from MIT Press.

Contributors xi

Jorge dos Reis
Assistant Professor, Faculty of Fine Arts, University of Lisbon, Portugal
Jorge dos Reis is a graphic designer. He was an apprentice typographic composer of a National Press first officer in the former Cais do Sodré Typography. He began his career by collaborating with the designer Robin Fior in Lisbon, Portugal, and with the typographer Alan Kitching in London, UK. He founded his own studio in 1996. His work is extensive and diverse, having a dual activity as a designer and as an artist: he makes graphic and typographic designs, exhibits drawings and paintings, and has published several books. He attended the National Conservatory in António Wagner's singing class studying with the composers Jorge Peixinho and Paulo Brandão while graduating in Communication Design at FBAUL, Lisbon. Jorge dos Reis has a Master of Arts from the Royal College of Art in London, a Master in Sociology of Communication from ISCTE, Lisbon, and a Doctorate from the University of Lisbon. He is currently an Assistant Professor at the Faculty of Fine Arts of the University of Lisbon, where he founded and directs the Master of Contemporary Typographic and Editorial Practice.

Caroline Archer-Parré
Professor of Typography, Centre for Printing History & Faculty of Art, Design & Media, Birmingham City University, UK
Caroline Archer-Parré is a Professor of Typography at Birmingham City University, Director of the Centre for Printing History and Culture (University of Birmingham/Birmingham City University), and Chairman of the Baskerville Society. She is the author of *The Kynoch Press, 1876-1982: the anatomy of a printing house* (British Library, 2000); *Paris Underground* (MBP, 2004); and *Tart cards: London's illicit advertising art* (MBP, 2003). Caroline is co-editor of *Beauty of Letters: Text, Type and Communication in the Eighteenth Century* (2020); *John Baskerville: Art and Industry of the Enlightenment* (2017); *Book 2.0: From Codex to the Computer* (2017); and *Religion and the Book Trade* (2015). She is Lead Series Editor on the Peter Lang Ltd series 'Printing History and Print Culture'.

Nuno Coelho
Assistant Professor, University of Coimbra, DEI, CEIS20 Research Center, Portugal
Nuno Coelho is a communication designer, an Assistant Professor of the Department of Informatics Engineering of the Faculty of Sciences and Technology of the University of Coimbra, and an Integrated Researcher at the Centre for 20th Century Interdisciplinary Studies of the University of Coimbra, Portugal.

xii *Contributors*

He holds a Ph.D. in Contemporary Art from the College of Arts of the University of Coimbra. He has a Masters in Design and Graphic Production from the Fine Arts School of the University of Barcelona, Spain, following completion of his degree course in Communication Design and Graphic Art at the Fine Arts School of the University of Porto, Portugal. As a Design researcher, he is interested in history, material culture, visual semiotics, and representation. He has curated and organized collective design exhibitions and public conferences. He has two books published.
https://apps.uc.pt/mypage/faculty/uc26736/en

Rúben Dias
Assistant Professor, ESAD, ESAD – Idea research center, Portugal

Rúben Dias has a PhD in Design and is Professor at ESAD, Matosinhos, Portugal. Internationally, he teaches workshops and is a speaker in type-related subjects. Rúben consulted and authored Manual do Tipógrafo and Imprimere's book and exhibition, promoted by ESAD–Idea, Matosinhos City Hall, and the Portuguese National Press – Mint House. With over two decades of experience, Rúben runs Itemzero, founded the letterpress workshop Tipografia Dias, and co-founded the collective Tipos das Letras. You can find more about Rúben on his website.

Sofia Meira
Invited Instructor, ESAD, ESAD–Idea research center, Portugal

Sofia Meira is a graphic designer based in Porto, Portugal, currently working at ESAD Matosinhos as a designer and printmaker. She graduated as a Master in Graphic Design at Escola Superior de Artes e Design – Caldas da Rainha 2014.She develops work and research in the area of Traditional Typography.

Catherine Dixon
Stage Leader, Graphic Communication Design Programme, Central Saint Martins, University of the Arts London, UK

Catherine Dixon is a designer, writer and teacher. She was appointed as research student to the project that made Typeform dialogues (Hyphen Press) and her doctoral thesis (2003) focused on the problems of describing typefaces. Her interest in typeface design is ongoing and she writes regularly for Fontstand and collaborates with several independent foundries, in addition to contributing to publications such as Matrix and Eye. She writes and presents regularly on letterpress as well as letterforms in environmental contexts, having co-authored with Phil Baines the book Signs: lettering in the environment. She is a Senior Lecturer and teaches typography on the Graphic Communication Design programme at Central Saint Martins where she also helps oversee the Central Lettering Record. From 2011to 2012, she was a Visiting Professor at the University of São Paulo in Brazil.

Roberto Gamonal Arroyo
Lecturer, Complutense University of Madrid, ES & EINA – University School of Design and Art, Barcelona, Spain
Roberto Gamonal Arroyo is a designer and teacher and academic researcher. He holds a Ph.D. in Applied Creativity and an MDes from the Faculty of Fine Arts UCM, Spain. He also has a BSc in Information from UCM, where he is currently an associate professor in the Department of Journalism II teaching courses related to communication design in journalism. He co-directs the MA "Editorial Design Print and Digital Media" and the specialization course "Design Typography" at the Istituto Europeo di Design – IED Madrid. In this center he also collaborates in teaching-related subjects in typography. He has been a Visiting Research Professor at the School of Design at the University of Guanajuato, Mexico, and the School of Applied Arts in Castelo Branco, Portugal. He belongs to the research groups Ciberimaginario and SOCMEDIA which bring his expertise in design to different research and development projects. He is also part of the editorial board of ICONO 14, a scientific journal dedicated to communication and emerging technologies. His research interests are directed at the contribution of design to other disciplines and establishing a discursive relationship with them. He is interested in both the most advanced and the oldest technologies of information and communication. The result of this is that he belongs to the groups UnosTiposDuros and Cultural Association Familia Plómez, that review the history of typography and composition techniques and printing craftsmanship.

Andreu Balius Planelles
Professor of Typography and Type Design, EINA – University School of Design and Art in Barcelona, Spain.
He holds a PhD in Design from the University of Southampton (UK). He is currently teaching typography and type design at EINA – University School of Design and Art in Barcelona. Andreu Balius is an award-winning typeface designer and runs his own studio, specialized in type design & typography in Barcelona. He has presented lectures and keynotes including at events such as ATypI conference (Helsinki, Finland, 2005; Lisbon, Portugal, 2006, and Mexico 2009), SND-ÑH (Lisbon, 2002), ImagineIT (Accademia di Belle Arti, Bologna, Italy, 2007), Bauhaus-Universität (Weimar, Germany, 2007), St Bride conference (Birmingham, UK, 2006), University of AppliedSciences and Arts of Southern Switzerland (Lugano,

Switzerland, 2007), and the International Type Conference in Valencia and Madrid (Spain, 2004, 2006).

Chris Wilson
Graduate Tutor, Visual Communications at Northumbria University, UK

Chris Wilson is a printmaker, design educator, and doctoral candidate based in Newcastle upon Tyne, UK. He is an award-winning innovation strategist, completing projects for a number of market-leading multinational companies. He is experienced in managing projects within a multidisciplinary team, acting as a consultant in areas of graphic design, service design, marketing, re-branding, and product development.

Since 2009, Wilson has operated as a freelance graphic designer and photographer, working for a diverse range of clients, producing identities, websites, promotions, and product photography.

He also works at Northumbria University at Newcastle in the School of Design as a graduate tutor. This involves the delivery of modules on the graphic design degree and research into post-digital letterpress printing.

Wilson continues to develop his own creative professional practice using a mixture of digital technologies and traditional crafts to produce printed artwork and graphic art.

Rita Carvalho
Assistant Professor, Lusófona University, DELLI / Centre for Other Worlds, Portugal

Rita Carvalho is Assistant Professor of Communication Design at DELLI and researcher at Centre for Other Worlds – Lusófona University, Lisbon, Portugal, developing experiences in Letterpress. She has a Ph.D. in Design by FAUL, Lisbon, with a thesis on illustration in a colonial context. She holds an MA in Visual Arts from the University of Évora, Portugal, with a project that intersects graffiti and medieval marginalia, and a degree in Communication Design from FBAUP, Porto, Portugal. Her main areas of interest are illustration, letterpress, graphic narratives, illumination and illustration history, and criticism. Since 2002 she has been working as a designer, illustrator, and graphic artist, with participation in various publications and exhibitions.

Amelia Hugill-Fontanel
RIT Cary Graphic Arts Collection, USA

Amelia Fontanel is a curator at the RIT Cary Graphic Arts Collection, Rochester, New York, USA, a renowned library that collects on design, typography, and the book arts. As manager of the Cary technology collection, she is responsible for teaching and maintaining some 23 different presses and thousands of fonts of metal and wood type. She is actively involved in the American letterpress community, holding board positions with the American Printing History Association and the Hamilton Wood Type and Printing Museum, Two Rivers, USA.

Richard Kegler
P22 Type Foundry, USA
Richard Kegler is the founder and lead designer of P22 Type Foundry. As a founder of the Western New York Book Arts Center in Buffalo, New York, Richard combined an interest in traditional crafts along with an entrepreneurial background to help create a self-sustaining community organization. The new P22 studio in Rochester, New York focuses on both digital and analog printing and typography.

Lucrezia Russo
Paris College of Art, France
Lucrezia Russo is an Italian graphic designer and educator, based in Paris, France.

She works for major French arts publishers and she is the Chair of the BFA in Communication Design at Paris College of Art.

Lucrezia holds an MA in Graphic Design (1998), Istituto Europeo di Design, Milan.

Her first publication, *The Nabokov Paper, an experiment in novel-reading*, co-conceived with Kate Briggs, was published in October 2013. Shandy Hall (Coxwold) hosted in November 2013 an eponymous exhibition, co-curated by Kate Briggs and Lucrezia Russo, to celebrate the book.

In 2013, she co-founded, with Céline Guyot and Andrew Schachman, Offschool, a structure exploring new forms of pedagogy in art, design, and architecture.

Ane Thon Knutsen
Oslo National Academy of The Arts, Norway
Ane Thon Knutsen is a graphic designer and artist living and working in Oslo, Norway.

She owns a private letterpress studio, teaches at Oslo National Academy of The Arts, does freelance lecturing, workshops, and is head of communication at Fellesverkstedet. In June 2019 she defended her PhD, *A Printing Press of One's Own*. Ane's expertise spans the wondrous possibilities of experimental printing, moveable type, artistic research, literature, bookmaking, tools, rooms, feminism and Virginia Woolf.

Erin Beckloff
Assistant Professor of Communication Design at Miami University, USA

Erin Beckloff is a letterpress printer, designer, educator, and filmmaker who preserves anecdotal and technical knowledge of printing history and culture. Her research explores the letterpress community's expansiveness through time and how the letterpress printing process will survive through educating others in the craft. She is the co-director and writer of "Pressing On: The Letterpress Film," a documentary about the survival of letterpress and the remarkable printers who preserve the history and knowledge of the craft.

She serves as an Assistant Professor of Communication Design at Miami University and holds an MFA in Graphic Design from Vermont College of Fine Arts, USA. In 2011 she revitalized the Curmudgeon Press type shop and developed letterpress courses as part of the Comm Design curriculum. She studies letterpress through practical application and the shared knowledge of master printers, including the talented folks at Hatch Show Print.

Erin disseminates her research through public and educational engagement. She has given presentations at two Hamilton Wood Type & Printing Museum Wayzgoose conferences; ATypI Antwerp; UCDA Design Education Summit; Type@Cooper New York; College Book Art Association Conferences; as well as taught workshops and lectured at universities across the USA and UK.

Acknowledgements

Writing and editing a collective authorship book on an evolving analog technology being practised in a digitally connected world is only possible due to the innumerous interactions and contributions of our friends, colleagues, and institutions that made this book possible.

First and foremost to our families for understanding and allowing us to invest the scarce time to develop this project. Also, the editors are profoundly grateful to the members of the letterpress community that has welcomed and nurtured our research so kindly. Many of them, from more than a dozen different countries, we are proud to be able to call friends today. A heartfelt acknowledgment to all the artists, researchers, printers, designers, and teachers who have submitted proposals to the call for works or who have organized activities within the programme of the PDLP: Post-Digital Letterpress Printing Conference that took place in Porto, Portugal, in January 2020 and that was at the origin of this book. Some of them are an important part of this book. Second to the members of the organization and programme committee of the conference – not only for their continuous support but also for their mentorship and engagement with this project. We would also like to thank the publisher, namely our editors, Isabella Vitti and Katie Armstrong, for believing and nurturing this into the final book form it assumes today.

Finally, we would like to recognize the support of our research institutes, the i2ADS Research Institute of Art, Design, and Society and the ID+ Research Institute for Design, Media, and Culture, both funded by grants from the FCT – Fundação para a Ciência e a Tecnologia, I.P., within the scope of the projects UIDP/04395/2020 and UIDB/04057/2020. This recognition is due not only for the logistic and organizational support to the research and events that led to this book but also for the kind financial support in the copy-editing of the final manuscript.

Foreword
After Quadrature: Concepts of Composition and Letterpress Forms

Johanna Drucker

Letterpress technology was invented in Germany in the mid-15th century. Until the coming of phototypesetting and computer-aided composition in the mid-20th century, letterpress remained, largely unchanged, as the method of print production in Western culture. Some automation occurred after the 1890s, and novel formats were also introduced in commercial work in the 19th century. But the technical affordances of letterpress printing drove, and even determined, its aesthetic features. The combination of the concepts of *quadrature* (squareness), *linearity*, and *modularity* became the conspicuous foundation of print design. These are embodied in the square metal bodies of the letters that were cast to facilitate their fitting into the bed. In spite of the long tradition of calligraphic expression in Korean, Chinese, and Japanese cultures, the casts produced for character-based printing also used the same format.

The conventions built into print (many adapted from manuscript features, but also subjected to a strict linear discipline) were carried over into photocomposition and digital technologies. The question is whether the conventions that became so firmly entrenched over five hundred years, and which codified many of the features present in manuscript production, are so engrained in the "programming" of literary work that even with the innovative capacity of digital tools, we are condemned to endless repetition of letterpress rules as the dominant terms of poetic imagination. Might the dialogue between digital tools and letterpress printing suggest other possibilities?

Before composing his radical *Un coup de dés jamais n'abolira le hazard* in the 1890s, the poet Stéphane Mallarmé bemoaned the "endless back and forth" repetition built into letterpress page, comparing it to the brutal action of beheading chickens. The image is stark. The poet feels the the sameness of the square, straight, line was as stifling to the imagination as an act of slaughter.

The history of writing in monumental inscriptions, manuscript traditions, and even ancient cuneiform and hieroglyphics is filled with examples of standardization and efficiency that reinforced linear approaches. The text of the Trajan column does not wander around in a non-linear way; nor do the monumental inscriptions of the city of Nineveh indulge in free-form design. To a great extent, the authority of written language depends on the fact that it appears to be "spoken", as if its utterances are unmarked, not situated in a specific human cultural frame. Writing seems to "speak" most authoritatively when it is least inflected by graphical markers.

Literature on the page is largely linear. The exceptions are conspicuous, classified as "visual" or "graphic" poetry, anomalies. As digital tools have replaced letterpress production, we can ask whether a dialogue between these methods can infuse imaginative innovation into the conception of literary works. What critical and conceptual potential does a 500-year-old technology have for informing, and literally giving new form to, poetic imagination?

Can letterpress printing be used as a medium of innovation? Is literary composition so conceptually integrated with the aesthetics of letterpress – as it has become embodied in digital platforms – that we cannot break free from it? Writing is conceived within forms. Digital formats that animate, morph, and play with the graphic design of text bring their own language to intellectual conception. Conforming to, or breaking from, formats can occur at the time of composition. More often, this occurs as a design "treatment" after a text is composed. The difference between these two is considerable. A treatment can inflect, reinforce, and massage a text. But to conceive a text within an alternative format requires internalization of the possibility in advance, as part of the conceptual composition process.

One may start with the type, its weight, size, and character in the resonant sense of letterforms. The arrangements can be freed from the "rule" that holds them – the metal bars that keep the letters aligned and tightly bound. They are the disciplinary agents of the hand-set type. Then remove them and skew the lines, and push the words into an unanticipated arrangement. But also consider the granular flexibility of manuscript calligraphy. In handwriting, everything is flexible, and the pen can insert new lines into old, smaller, and larger letters into an ordered or disordered array. Recall the hand-drawn exemplars of master calligraphers such as the 16th-century masterwork by Georg Bocskay, *Mira Calligraphiae Monumenta*. The exquisite lettering appeared in engraved plates and later in lithographic work. Graphical imagination fed by hand has the capacity to alter the writing mind.

Digital technology has not freed us from the constraints of letterpress, cast metal, or quadrature. Perversely, letterpress production itself offers real possibilities to rethink inherited conventions that have constrained digital formats within longstanding legacies. These technologies may also benefit by being informed by the flexibility of the ductal imagination, the fluidity of the pen and hand that traces thought forms into existence as a graphical language. The mind thinks from the hand and eye, and not merely through them as instruments of already-formed expression.

Introduction

*Pedro Amado, Ana Catarina Silva
and Vítor Quelhas*

During its centuries-old history, letterpress printing has recorded several milestones, both as a commercial endeavour and as a cultural driver of modern civilisation, attaining its peak in the early twentieth century. Due to technological developments such as photocomposition and digital printing from the late twentieth century onwards, letterpress, as a professional activity, has slowly waned. In recent years, it has been the object of artistic exploration and speculative design within personal or commercial contexts. Research projects also aim to reflect on the methods, strategies, and challenges within the framework of a craft-based local economy that is currently on the decline.

Since the *end of letterpress printing* as a commercial endeavour, we have witnessed its second life as a global trend. Several initiatives have appeared worldwide, fuelling a continuous interest in exploring this technology. These range from historical research to design applications, including artistic, activist, and educational initiatives; and from local or individual showcases to international exhibitions using traditional or innovative approaches (e.g. the *Reverting to Type* international exhibition of protest posters and TIPO um Encontro de Impressores Tipográficos [TIPO – A Meeting of Letterpress Printers]). Research conferences (e.g. the Letterpress Printing: Past, Present, Future conference), practice-based symposiums (e.g. Letterpress Workers), educational-oriented conferences (e.g. Make Ready Symposium for Letterpress Educators) and recently formed associations (e.g. Letterpress Educators of Art & Design).

This book presents a sample of cases that illustrate this reality. Work from printers, designers, educators, and researchers who at the same time are practitioners of this medium, in the current post-digital design contexts. Digital technology is no longer a revolutionary phenomenon but a normal part of everyday life, where transitions from digital to analogue are common in both directions, giving rise to new hybrid and valuable artefacts and processes. Contemporary designers and printers sample, remix, and mash-up these analogue and digital techniques in innovative processes and creative experimental results.

The motivation and origin of this book spawned from the organisation and participation in multiple international events and exhibitions. But why write such a book today, when this phenomenon has been going on for at least three decades? Over recent years, digital fabrication tools have become more accessible. As the fusion between atoms and bits becomes more pervasive, traditional printers and digital designers blur the boundaries between their processes and breathe a new life into letterpress printing by introducing new materials, such as resin, methacrylate, MDF or plastic. These are used alongside traditional metal or wood sorts, in flatbed or cylindrical presses, or even with experimental printing presses. Studios, such as the p98a or the P22, and individuals such as Dafi Kühne or Ryan Molloy are living and thriving examples of using a hybrid mix of traditional and custom-built tools that explore the limits of this medium. But the current generation of graphic designers is the first to no longer have professors or contact with technicians who were formally trained in traditional letterpress. Their legacy and added value are in danger of being lost. It is therefore paramount to actively improve the pedagogy and practice of graphic design. Research on how to incorporate letterpress practices and processes today provides the ground to rethink the creative and technological advances, as well as the impact, caused by the ubiquity of digital tools in our daily lives. From revisiting traditional methods to emulating or exploring beyond the limits of new materials and digitally enabled processes, letterpress research and its interpretations in contemporary art and design practice not only go beyond specialist research into printing history and technology but also cross the design and fine arts practices. The result of these initiatives stimulates the engagement of an international community of researchers and practitioners with the idiosyncrasies of the current post-digital culture.

The argument presented throughout this book is three-fold. Firstly, letterpress, as a technology for cultural expression, is a rich field for social and historical research since it produces cultural artefacts that record social values, prejudices, forms of expression, and aesthetics, encapsulated over time. Secondly, as a technology that has been used in educational contexts over time, it is important to analyse and reflect on the different pedagogical approaches and benefits in the education of designers and artists, especially in the conflict that arises from the different fields of study. What were once domains restricted to each field's gatekeepers now constitute fertile ground for hybrid innovation. Thirdly, contemporary letterpress practices are explored by printers, makers, designers, and educators in their ongoing work, or pedagogical practices, contributing not only to the revival of letterpress—maintaining its legacy—but most importantly sustaining its evolution. This book is organised into three parts: Part I—Research—highlights the contribution of letterpress to the fields of arts and design research. It acknowledges that letterpress plays a relevant role within social, aesthetic, and human expression. Part II—Education—presents the relationship between letterpress practice and design education. It considers the current unique pedagogical challenges, both in academic circles and in professional contexts. Part III—Practice—discloses current letterpress practices by different artists, designers, and makers. These accounts report to a future view of the letterpress practice, bringing it closer to the individual designer and maker.

Part I
Introduction
Research

This part highlights a reflection on the contribution made by letterpress to the arts and design research field. It is seen through the lens of four case studies that explore the cultural legacy of letterpress communication artifacts within commercial and artistic production contexts.

It acknowledges that letterpress plays a relevant role within cultural and aesthetic expectations—ranging from the fields of archival collections, printing and design history to practice-based artistic research—that often include considerations of social, aesthetic, and human factors.

This first contribution highlights the evolution of a typeface design over a century. Amelia Hugill-Fontanel traces the various permutations of Cloister Initials, from its beginning as a metal typeface, through digital versions, and back into physical forms, demonstrating that letterforms currently transcend digital and material formats.

The following chapter considers the work of those who appropriated printing from the external expanding possibilities. Caroline Archer considers how these typographic outsiders equipped themselves with the knowledge and skills to become printers, what they produced, and what lessons they can offer today's artists and designers entering the field of letterpress.

The second chapter explores the relationship between the creative process and letterpress printing methods, focusing on the life and work of a Portuguese designer from the mid-twentieth century. Nuno Coelho starts by analyzing the designer's influences and creative process and then focuses on his packaging designs. More than technological constraints, the chapter emphasizes the influence of cultural heritage on the graphic design of consumer products.

The third chapter presents a recent practice-based research project in hybrid letterpress printing. Ane Thon Knutsen, a female self-taught printer, explains how crucial the material conditions for artistic practice are to artistic autonomy. Analyzing Virginia Woolf's *The Mark on The Wall*, she reshapes the original experience acknowledging the role played by the printing press as her road to freedom.

DOI: 10.4324/9781003173113-1

Part I
Research Highlight
The Seven Lives of a Typeface: Material and Immaterial Convergences

Amelia Hugill-Fontanel[1]

> *Understanding excellent designs from the past in such analytical terms, rather than simply regarding them as graphic images to fetishize, is the challenge—when we do it, we can learn from the past.*
>
> (Luna, 2019, p. 129)[2]

As printing historians, we explore motives, materials, and technologies that have contributed to the primary technology of mass communication for five centuries: printing. It is thrilling to share in-depth research, especially when tangible typographic objects are the results of the effort. The cycle of research, ideation, and production repeats, where the past feeds present and future practice. This is an account that documents how a typeface design enjoyed at least seven reincarnations during a 100-year period of technological innovation, culminating in contemporary creative graphic work.

The American type designer Frederic W. Goudy (1865–1947), designed over 120 letterpress typefaces in his long career. Cary Graphic Arts Collection at Rochester Institute of Technology holds significant archival material by Goudy, including correspondence and typeface drawings, photographs, books, and even types that he cast and the printing presses that he owned. Goudy's work is ubiquitous in the digital landscape due to the fact that the revival of *Goudy Old Style* is commonly bundled as a system font on international operating systems.

In 1917 Frederic Goudy drew a floriated Capital A in the style of medieval manuscript historiated initial letters for his book, *The Alphabet*.[3] The director of American Type Founders (ATF) convinced Goudy to draw the

DOI: 10.4324/9781003173113-2

full alphabet for commercial release as a hot metal letterpress 'typeface.' This became his 33rd design, entitled *Cloister Initials*. It was cast in display sizes from 48- to 144-point. Enjoying prominent use through the 1940s, ATF kept it in production for years as a foundry type.

Writing a few decades after their creation, Goudy noted that the *Cloister Initials* 'have had a long and useful life and are still extensively used and copied.'[4] He was alluding to their popularity and inclination to be pirated by competing typefounders. He permitted translations of this design himself. For example, in the 1930s they were rebranded as *Goudy Initials, no. 296* for the automated typecasting system from Lanston Monotype Machine Company. Hence the first and second 'lives' of *Cloister Initials* were personally monitored by their creator.

The mid-twentieth-century evolution of myriad type production modes incited many older designs to be adapted to new technologies. From the 1960s to the 1980s *Cloister Initials* were translated into phototype as well as dry-transfer letters. With the introduction of digital typefaces, they became one of the early candidates for revival. The alphabet's designs were digitized as individual EPS files by Gerald Giampa when he purchased the remnants of the Lanston Company in the late 1980s.[5] *Cloister Initials*' third, fourth, and fifth lives were mediocre surrogates for the elegant letterpress-printed originals. Phototypesetting's ability to optically resize and compress characters, as well as early digital jagged type vectors, contributed to this inferior quality.

Lanston's intellectual property was acquired in 2004 by P22 Type Foundry of Buffalo, New York. They redrew the *Cloister Initials* in 2005 and reformatted the EPS files to digital font formats, renaming them as *LTC Goudy Initials*. In 2014, P22 decided to rework the typeface from the most accurate source material.[6] This involved a fortuitous discovery of the original 120-point ATF brass matrices at the RIT Cary Graphic Arts Collection.[7] An RIT curator had rescued the mats from the salvage auction when ATF was in bankruptcy liquidation in 1993.[8] This sixth digital incarnation of the typeface was poised to rejoin the analogue world.

RIT loaned the *Cloister Initials* 120-point matrices to Richard Kegler of P22 for the purposes of casting a new metal type. Only one machine in North America could handle the work, due to the fact that the matrices are such a large point size. This was the last extant Giant Pivotal caster, which was coincidentally sold to a fellow buyer at the 1993 ATF auction: printer and typecaster, Gregory Walters in Ohio.[9] Casting with this machine was not an automated process, since each mould needed to be manually disconnected from its housing to eject the type.[10] After several days of involved labour, Walters and Kegler were able to cast a few dozen complete alphabets of Goudy's almost century-old typeface. Each character weighed 0.75 pounds (0.34 kg).

Since 2014, *Cloister Initials* has enjoyed its seventh life as an analogue/digital hybrid. The 120-point metal recasting sold out quickly to print shops in the United States and Europe. P22's enhanced digital type revival added the functionality of chromatic accents to Goudy's original design, with separate fonts that isolated inline character fills and the floriated backgrounds.[11] These font files were recently used in 2020 to fabricate analogue letterpress plates through computer-aided design applications.[12]

Digital processes have influenced letterpress plate production since the early 1990s,[13] with the use of flexographic relief photopolymer and photo-etched magnesium or zinc plates. These standardised processes join a fertile ground for experimentation in contemporary digital laser-engraved and 3D-printed plates. Using *Cloister Initials* designs, several comparative characters were made with all of these technologies in a collaboration between P22 Type Foundry and RIT Cary Graphic Arts Collection. They were printed using a Vandercook cylinder printing press at P22 (Figure P1.1).

The printed comparisons from digitally fabricated plates were promising. Photopolymer plates are known for the ability to render accurate detail in letterpress prints at small sizes. Fine tolerances in plate production at a

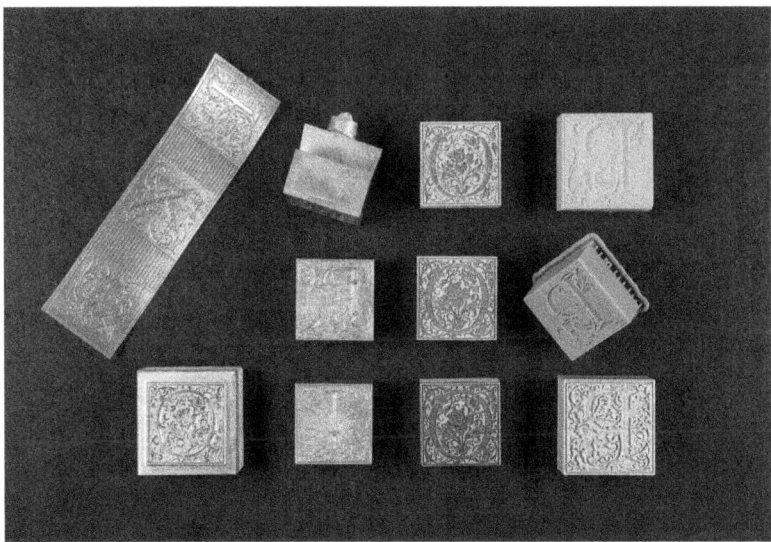

Figure P1.1 Letterpress Type. From Right Column, Top to Bottom: Goudy Cloister Initials Relief Type in Photopolymer; Photo-Etched Magnesium; Modern Lead-Alloy Cast from Original Brass Matrices; Laser-Engraved Maple Wood; Stereolithographic Plastic; Fused Deposition Model 3D Print. Photograph by Jiageng Lin.

service bureau and the careful machining of their aluminium printing base make photopolymer plates predictable printing matrices.[14] This was true for the *Cloister Initials* test, with no surprise. The etched magnesium plate also printed well but had more variance in the type height of its plywood-mounted base which had to be corrected in proofing.[15] In this way, the photopolymer and magnesium plates joined the P22-cast metal sort in a control group of acceptable prints.

The laser-engraved *Cloister Initials* character yielded high-quality detail in the floral tendril shapes that replicated the control group's results. However, this fineness was a direct result of the quality of the wood from which it was cut. This was end-grain maple hardwood that had been carefully milled to letterpress height and face-sanded and shellacked before engraving. All of this work depended greatly on the skill of the worker who prepared the wood—a resource that is not accessible to all. Laser-engraving also requires a lot of testing to refine the laser's kerf or cutting width, so that the relief block may approximate a piece of cast type.[16]

Encouraging results were derived from the stereolithographic 3D printing process. This makes 3D objects by successively 'printing' or depositing thin layers using a liquid plastic medium that is curable by ultraviolet light. The Formlabs' Form 3 SLA printer built a *Cloister Initials* character with a resolution of 50 microns per layer starting from the bottom foot to the type's face. The letterform curves were acceptably maintained, but a faint striated pattern was apparent in the positive or solid black portions of the 3D-printed type. This would be considered a defect in a cast piece of metal type.

A failed experiment in additive printing used Fused Deposition Modelling (FDM). Here a filament of a thermoplastic material was fed from a coil through a moving, heated extruder head and deposited on the growing work. The FDM 3D printer could not produce a filament that was thin enough to replicate *Cloister Initials*' intricate scrollwork.[17]

It is important to underscore that the *Cloister Initials*' seventh life in the current post-digital environment is non-binary, in terms of being material (analogue) *versus* immaterial (digital).[18] It embraces a hybrid existence where one mode of creation blurs seamlessly into another. While Goudy drew his inspiration from media that predates movable type printing, his designs have complexity that tests the limits of contemporary technologies. If one were to forecast into the future at the end of the post-digital period, perhaps in 2035—when type moves unguided on the screen or is converted to 3D effortlessly in several media—Goudy's *Cloister Initials* will have perhaps twice as many lives to be documented with a timelessness that transcends any given format.

Notes

1. This work was first presented with Richard Kegler of P22 Type Foundry at the 2020 Post-Digital Letterpress Conference in Porto, Portugal. The author wishes to acknowledge his continued collaboration, especially in editing this article.
2. Paul Luna, *Typography, A Very Short Introduction* (Oxford: Oxford University Press, 2019): 129.
3. Frederic W. Goudy, *The Alphabet: Fifteen Interpretative Designs Drawn and Arranged with Explanatory Text and Illustrations* (New York: Mitchell Kennerley, 1918).
4. Frederic W. Goudy, *Half-Century of Type and Typography 1895–1945*, vol. 1 (New York: The Typophiles, 1945).
5. Giampa Textware/Lanston Type Co. Vancouver, Canada, 1991.
6. 'Goudy Initials,' P22 Type Foundry. https://p22.com/family-Goudy_Initials.
7. Richard Kegler, 'Goudy Cloister Initials,' *Devil's Artisan*, no.86, Spring/Summer 2020, http://devilsartisan.ca/p22_type_specimens_goudy_cloister_in itials.html.
8. David Pankow, 'The Rise and Fall of ATF.' *Printing History* 22, nos. 43/44 (2002): 3–14.
9. P22 Type Foundry, 'Casting Metal Type: Cloister Initials,' *Adobe Behance*, 2014, https://www.behance.net/gallery/17665337/Casting-Metal-Type-Cloister-Initials.
10. The Giant pivotal casting work was dangerous too, as molten lead could accidentally squirt under high pressure when it was injected into a matrix.
11. 'LTC Goudy Initials Fill' and 'LTC Goudy Initials Flora,' P22 Type Foundry. https://p22.com/family-Goudy_Initials.
12. Amelia Hugill-Fontanel and Richard Kegler, 'The Seven Lives of a Typeface,' presentation, Porto, Portugal: *Post Digital Letterpress Printing*, January 31, 2020.
13. Betty Bright, 'Letterpress in the Second Millennium,' in *Fine & Dirty: Contemporary Letterpress Art* (Minneapolis, MN: Center for Book Arts, 2012): 6.
14. Boxcar Press of Syracuse, New York manufactured the photopolymer plate from digital files supplied by the authors in early 2020. https://www.boxcarpress.com.
15. Hodgins Engraving of Batavia, New York, supplied the service of making photo-etched magnesium plates. http://www.hodginsengraving.com.
16. Scott Moore of Moore Wood Type in Ohio made the laser-cut *Cloister Initials* blocks from digital files. https://moorewoodtype.com.
17. The 3D-printed type was made at the RIT College of Art and Design FabLab. https://confluence.cad.rit.edu/cadtech/cad-fablab.
18. Jeremy Knox, 'What Does the "Postdigital" Mean for Education? Three Critical Perspectives on the Digital, with Implications for Educational Research and Practice,' *Postdigital Science and Education* 1 (2019): 357–370, https://doi.org/10.1007/s42438-019-00045-y.

1 Appropriating Printing

Caroline Archer-Parré

For much of the seventeenth century, from 1637 to 1695, printing in England was controlled by statutes and laws which not only regulated the number of presses and printers that could operate in the country, but also determined what could, and could not, be produced.[1] The Acts and Decrees enacted by Parliament were a response to a widely-held fear that the freedom to print was a threat to society, a challenge to the crown, and a danger to the Church. But it was not just Acts of Parliament that hampered engagement with printing: so too did the trade's rigid structure and organisation. From the time William Caxton (1422–91)[2] introduced printing into England in 1476 no one was able to set up as a Master Printer without having served an apprenticeship. Master Printers defended their privileges and protected their skills,[3] and it was only they, assisted perhaps by a journeyman or apprentice, who could issue printed material.[4] The terms of apprenticeship were enshrined in law and first regulated by the Statute of Artificers (1563 and 1601), which authorised and made national that which had been usual practice.[5] Later, the printing trade unions also exerted tight controls over who and how many people could join the trade, and what they could do.[6] Just as parliament had imposed restrictions on the printing trade, so the trade itself enforced tight controls on who could join it. The controlled became the controller and as a consequence printing was almost impenetrable to those outsiders who wished to engage with the craft whether for pleasure or for profit.[7]

This chapter considers the work of those who, over the course of 500 years, have circumvented the system, operated outside trade conventions, and appropriated printing for their own purposes. Some were private individuals who participated in the craft either for leisure or pleasure; writers who turned to the medium to promote their literary endeavours; or pirate-printers who used the process for the production of fakes and fabrications, seditious and illicit literature. This chapter looks at how these typographic outsiders equipped themselves with the necessary knowledge and skills to operate their presses, considers what they produced, and reflects on their reasons for so doing.

Printing at Home: From Palaces to Parlours

In the early eighteenth century, in the new era of comparative press freedom, individuals from outside the trade began to appropriate the press and print from their own homes, in order to fill their leisure time. It is a habit that persists today. Twenty-first-century home-printers adopt historical typographic technology to print for pleasure; and nearly everyone has a home computer which has placed the typographer's tools-of-the-trade in the hands of the everyman. In the eighteenth and nineteenth centuries, so many people took to printing that it soon became the craft most widely pursued by amateurs.[8] These home-based printers operated outside the constraints of the trade; they were lay enthusiasts who were usually—but not always—male, wealthy, generally well-educated, and primarily interested in the products of the press rather than the mechanics of the process.[9] By printing poems and prose of their own authorship, or written by their friends, they were 'vanity' printers who established their own private presses and employed the skills of professional compositors and pressmen to reproduce their literary endeavours. Probably the best known eighteenth-century home-printer was the historian, politician, and man of letters, Horace Walpole (1717–97).[10] Walpole established his Strawberry Hill Press in 1757 at Twickenham, Surrey where he employed a single man to act as both compositor and pressman, to help print works of his own creation and those written by his friend, the poet Thomas Gray.[11] The English bibliographer and genealogist Sir Samuel Egerton Brydges (1762–1837) recruited the services of the printers John Johnson and John Warwick to help produce his many volumes of literature at his Lee Priory Press, Kent.[12] In addition, the English journalist, and radical politician John Wilkes (1725–97) briefly kept, in 1763, a large-scale printing office in his house in Great George Street, London, where he had two presses and eight men working for him.[13] So large was the set-up that, in order to accommodate the presses, Wilkes had to 'call in carpenters to enlarge the hall'.[14]

Space and financial resources were the greatest deterrents for most aspiring eighteenth-century home-printers. Pressmen had to be paid, and typographic machinery was prohibitively large and cumbersome[15] so the home-printer needed both a bank account and a house sufficiently large to accommodate the workers and material necessary for production. To satiate the needs of the home-printer, scaled-down presses were designed, manufactured, and sold specifically for amateurs who could operate them at home, without employing the assistance of a trade printer. The London engraver

Appropriating Printing 11

and etcher, John Sutter, first advertised his portable press in 1769 for use by 'noblemen, gentlemen, and ladies curious in printing'.[16] Sutter had competition. John Brown first manufactured a 'Portable-Printing Press' in around 1770 and used it to print his own writings.[17] Interest in scaled-down presses started with royalty. In England the Duke of Cumberland and his sisters printed works using a portable press at St James's Palace in 1713.[18] In France Louis XIV (1638–1715) reputedly printed on a scaled-down press.[19] Once French royalty involved themselves with printing it was only a matter of time before other members of the Court took an interest in the craft. The Marquis de Marigny (1727–81) printed from his home in Bercy.[20] There is no evidence of what, if anything, Marigny printed, but his curiosity was primarily linked to the science, technology, and mechanics of printing. By contrast, Marigny's sister, Jeanne Antoinette Poisson (1721–64), better known as Madame de Pompadour), was concerned with the artistic potential of the craft and was taught etching by the French painter, François Boucher (1703–70) under whose guidance she created fifty-two engravings of his drawings.[21] Pompadour also developed an interest in typographic printing,[22] and kept a scaled-down wooden press on which, it may be presumed, she printed works of her own composition.[23]

It was, perhaps, inevitable that once Kings and their Courts had taken up printing, it should filter down through the classes and become 'a polite study for humble patrons and people of more leisure'.[24] By the nineteenth century, printing was adopted by the middle-classes as an affordable, satisfying, and intellectually profitable pastime: 'there is probably no art or science calculated to afford so much gratification to amateurs as printing, inasmuch as it is a valuable handmaid or assistant to all other arts'.[25] As a result, a trend in home-printing became popular with the middle-classes who started to use their leisure time to print calling cards, invitations for parties, or small publications of their own composition for private circulation. So large was the community of home-printers that by the mid-nineteenth century a number of companies, including Holtzapffel & Co., tool and lathe makers, London, were designing, manufacturing and commercially retailing 'toy' printing presses specifically for their needs.[26]

The endeavours of the home-printer were supported by a range of literature. In 1864 David Garden Berri published *The Art of Printing*.[27] Aimed at popularising the typographic arts amongst the general public it sought to enable anyone, through a few simple instructions, to become their own printer. *The Art of Printing* was followed by several other illustrated guides, culminating with P. E. Raynor's popular *Printing for Amateurs* (1875).[28] Designed for the layman, these volumes contained practical details on the machinery and materials required for printing, together with descriptions of the processes necessary for their handling. The fact that so many books on printing were published and republished in the mid-nineteenth century demonstrates that there was a marked demand for typographic instruction from a public interested in doing it themselves. This literature is still available to the current generation of home-printers, but the Internet provides more interactive instructions, including videos on sites such as YouTube.

Just as nineteenth-century home-printers enjoyed seeing the products of their pens realised in print, so too did more established twentieth-century authors. V. S. Naipaul (1932–2018), James Herbert (1943–2013), and Terry Pratchett (1948–2015) each took an interest in how their words were reproduced and worked closely with their printers on the typographic presentation of their texts. Other authors, however, took production, quite literally, into their own hands by printing their own material. Virginia Woolf (1882–1941)[29] and her husband Leonard (1880–1969),[30] founded the Hogarth Press in 1917 as a diversion from the pressures of writing. Starting with a small hand-press at their Surrey home, they not only printed Virginia's own work, but also that of other writers such as Katherine Mansfield, T. S. Eliot, C. Day-Lewis, and E. M. Forster. In addition, the Woolfs' press provided avenues of expression for many artists, photographers, illustrators and designers. Following the success of *Kew Gardens* in 1919 the Hogarth Press evolved into a commercial enterprise.[31] In 1946 it was sold to the publishers Chatto & Windus. The Hogarth Press, which had started as a diversion and escape from mainstream publishing, became a victim of its own success and succumbed to the commercial pressures which it had been established to avoid. In his autobiography, *Good-Bye to All That*,[32] Robert Graves (1895–1985),[33] a friend and contemporary of Woolf, described how 'In 1927 [he] began learning to print on a hand-press. In 1928 [he] continued learning to print'.[34] Graves, together with the poet Laura Riding (1901–91),[35] founded the Seizin Press in London. Graves knew many people in the printing trade and his typographically-aware friend, the author Vyvyan Richards, taught him to compose type using a Monotype caster and how to print on an 1872 Crown Albion Press. The Seizin Press enabled Graves and Riding to print their own work, including Riding's first book of poetry, *Love as Love, Death as Death*, free from the constraints of publishers.[36]

Both the Hogarth and Seizin Presses used historical typographic equipment on which to print their publications. At the turn of the twentieth century, printing was moving from a craft-based trade to a technology-led industry. Letterpress printing was giving way to offset lithography, hand composition to mechanical typesetting. The modern mechanical composing machines and printing presses were larger, more expensive and required specialist training to operate in contrast to the old hand-operated presses which were simpler to operate and maintain. As mechanisation became more prevalent, so too did union restrictions on who could and could not operate the machines.[37] As trade printers began jettisoning the old technology in favour of the new, their redundant equipment became available to home-printers, who, like Woolf and Graves, appropriated it for their own purposes. Some authors preferred, however, to appropriate contemporary printing presses. Aldous Huxley (1894–1965),[38] for example, was interested in using modern printing machinery to provide high-quality books for the masses and wrote much on the subject.[39] But by-and-large home-printers appropriated historical printing equipment. It is a trend that persists today, as contemporary home-printers eschew modern technology in favour of historical equipment, drawn to the tactility of the process, the materiality of the operation, and the olfactory delight of ink and oils. There is also the satisfaction in having rescued, restored and brought back to life machines of a by-gone era, salvaging the past to serve the present: a sentiment that chimes with current environmental concerns to reuse and recycle resources.

Printing in Private: Pirates and Pornographers

Home-printers operate in full sight of the law and with the knowledge—and disapproval[40]—of the trade. Pirate-printers, on the other hand, worked out of sight of the authorities and without the sanction of the trade, in order to produce fakes, forgeries and other typographic fabrications. The fear of forgery was one of the reasons behind the 1637 Star Chamber Decree which was also designed to prevent 'abuses in printing seditious, treasonable and unlicensed books and pamphlets, printing and printing presses'. For centuries, however, everything from counterfeit banknotes to philatelic forgeries and seditious literature has been produced surreptitiously, and in defiance of Decrees and trade unions, either by fully indentured trade printers turned criminals, or by crooks using unlicensed pirate presses.

Seditious libel, printed in order to subvert the State or incite discontent, was produced behind firmly closed doors, usually by politically motivated or doctrinally sympathetic pirate-printers. In 1683, for example, John Culefant, whose regular profession is unknown, was convicted of offences against the King when he was tried for printing, and publishing, two scandalous and seditious libels: *The growth of popery*, and *Ignoramus Justice*.[41] Culefant not only printed the material but also commissioned the copy, corrected the proofs, and encouraged the work. At his trial he was found guilty, fined and pilloried. Similarly, John Lowthorp, a clergyman by profession, was indicted in 1690 for a 'high misdemeanour, in writing, printing and publishing a most pernicious, scandalous, seditious and notorious libel against the King and Government'.[42] Lowthorp was stripped of the cloth and fined, and his books were burnt by the Common Hangman at Westminster.[43] So seriously did the State take the role of the printer, that in 1675 one nameless convict, a scrivener by trade, was not only accused of printing scandalous libels but also for being 'a pretended printer'. He was fined, imprisoned and prohibited from 'exercising or using the trade of printing for three years to come'.[44]

Forgery was particularly rampant in the late eighteenth century when, for the first time, the Bank of England issued low-denomination notes that were handled by people unaccustomed to paper currency and often illiterate.[45] They were the natural victims of forgers.[46] In 1789, for example, newspapers widely reported the arrest of three men in Dublin caught printing fake one guinea notes.[47] Counterfeiting was widespread and producing forgeries remained a lucrative trade for pirate-printers despite punitive penalties. In the eighteenth century anyone interested in calling on one of London's brothels could buy a guidebook, *Harris' List of Covent Garden Ladies* (1758-95), to help them find a lady suitable to their needs. Published pseudonymously and printed illicitly by John and James Roach and John Aitkin, their covert operations took place in plain sight and alongside their legitimate work in their printing house in Covent Garden, London. An echo of *Harris' Guide* was heard two centuries later in 1961 when an enterprising pornographer, Frederic Shaw, published in London a *Ladies Directory*.[48] Shaw was indicted for 'conspiracy to corrupt public morals', convicted and sentenced. Shaw was part of Britain's thriving mid-twentieth century underground press movement, which promoted anti-establishment ideas, allied itself with the hippy drug-inspired culture and championed a new age of sexual freedom. Publications included *International Times* (1966–72) and the Marxist paper *Black Dwarf* (1968–70). Perhaps the most influential was *Oz* magazine (1967–73). Published monthly by Richard Neville (1941–2016),[49] and achieving an average circulation of 30,000 copies, it became the chief organ of the British underground press movement. Renowned for its graphic invention and its constantly changing format, *Oz*'s printers took full advantage of new printing stocks, including metallic foils, new fluorescent inks and the greater flexibility of layout offered by offset lithography. The magazine gained notoriety for its editorial policies and the forthright manner in which it tackled sex. But it was a cartoon image of a priapic Rupert Bear that caused particular consternation with the authorities. *Oz*'s printing works were raided; its publishers were taken for trial and indicted for corrupting the morals of children and young people.

London's underground press did not end with the *Oz* trial, and there is still a flourishing network of pirate-printers prepared to run the gauntlet of the authorities and print the material the police would rather see banned. Probably the most apparent products of the underground press are London's 'tart cards' (1984–today) which appear in telephone boxes around the capital, advertising the services of the city's prostitutes.[50] Produced by an

Appropriating Printing 15

established circle of underground printers, the early cards were manufactured on a range of obsolete equipment. Initially, type was created on a kitchen table using cut-out letters or rub-down characters such as Letraset; later word-processing systems drove low-quality bubble-jet printers, followed by personal computers which placed the typographer's tools-of-the-trade in the hands of the everyman. Printing was usually undertaken using offset lithography and occasionally letterpress by an established circle of pirate-printers working from unspecified addresses away from the centre of the city in order to avoid arousing the curiosity of the authorities.

Conclusion

Home-printers and pirate-printers, whether working in the fifteenth or twentieth century, had much in common. Both parties were dependent upon access to obsolete equipment. Home-printers used old machinery because government decrees and trade union rules, coupled with financial constraints, prohibited them from using current materials. In addition, technically advanced machines usually occupied more space and required greater skill to operate than historical equipment: both of which were beyond the average home-printer. Similarly, pirate-printers were often forced to work with antiquated machinery because it was cheap to purchase, and because its obsolescence may have rendered it unlicensed and therefore almost untraceable either by the trade or the authorities. For the wealthy home-printer, learning to operate the equipment was done under the guidance of a trade printer; but most home-printers were self-taught and simply followed the instructions provided by manufacturers manuals, or were guided by one of the many publications produced on the subject. Most pirate-printers, on the other hand, were indentured trade printers turned criminals, who simply transferred their skills across technologies. But whether home-printers or pirate-printers, their motivations for taking to the press are curiously similar. Each was inspired by the freedom to print whatever they wanted, the liberty to distribute their words to whom they wanted, and to appropriate typographic control—for better or for worse—for the everyman.

Today we are all typographers thanks to the advent of personal computers and the arrival of desktop printers. Such equipment has not only placed the typographer's tools-of-the-trade in the hands of everyone, it has also emancipated the printed word and appropriated it for the purposes of the digital era. Never in the history of printing have individuals experienced so much freedom to express themselves, with so much control on how they communicate, both in public and in private, or been able to do so at speed. They have done so without knowledge of printing, the hindrance of large expensive equipment, or having to engage the services of a printing professional. Now everyone can control their typographic identity, whether to produce the mundane—such as newsletters, stationery, invitation cards—or the exotic, as seen in the large-scale digital typographic representations created by the artists Gilbert & George.[51] Both the mundane and the exotic serve to demonstrate how specialised production equipment has ceased to be the exclusive tool of pre-press experts and become an instrument in the hand of the artist. However, the speed, freedom and comparative cheapness of digital reproduction has also initiated a resurgence of interest in mechanical process, and old typographic technologies have been made new again in the hands of a new generation of artists and designers, whose unfettered imaginations produce work that would have been unimaginable to their predecessors in print.

Notes

1 Star Chamber Decree (1637); 'Act for preventing abuses in printing seditious, treasonable and unlicensed books and pamphlets, printing and printing presses' (1662). Raymond Astbury, 'The renewal of the licensing act in 1693 and its lapse in 1695', *The Library* 5, 1978, iv, 298–322.
2 N. F. Blake, 'Caxton, William (1415 x 24–1492), printer, merchant, and diplomat', *Oxford dictionary of national biography* (Oxford, 2008). Online, https://0-www-oxforddnb-com.catalogue.wellcomelibrary.org/view/10.1093/ref:odnb/9780198614128.001.0001/odnb-9780198614128-e-4963, accessed 18 January 2021.
3 David Jury, *Graphic design before graphic designers: the printer as designer and craftsman, 1700–1914* (London, 2012), 15–16.
4 T. A. Skingsley, 'Technical training and education in the English printing industry', *Printing Historical Society Journal* 13, 1978/9, 1–25.
5 Skingsley, 'Technical training'.
6 Skingsley, 'Technical training'.
7 Caroline Archer-Parré, 'Private pleasures and portable presses: do-it-yourself printers in the eighteenth century', in C. Archer-Parré & M. Dick (eds) *Pen, print and communication in the eighteenth century* (Liverpool, 2020), 89–106.
8 R. Cave, *The private press* (London, 1971); Jeremy Black, *The English press in the eighteenth century* (Abingdon, 2011).
9 Robert Stebbins, *Amateurs, professionals and serious leisure* (Montreal, 1992).
10 Michael Snodin & Cynthia E Roman, *Horace Walpole's Strawberry Hill* (London & New Haven, CT, 2009).
11 James Mosley, 'The press in the parlour: some notes on the amateur printer and his equipment', *The Black Art* 2, 1962, i, 1–15.
12 K. A. Manley, 'Brydges, Sir (Samuel) Egerton, first baronet, styled thirteenth Baron Chandos', *Oxford dictionary of national biography*. Online, doi.org/10.1093/ref:odnb/3809, accessed 14 June 2019.
13 P. Thomas, 'Wilkes, John (1725–97), politician', *Oxford dictionary of national biography*. Online, https://www.oxforddnb.com/view/10.1093/ref:odnb/9780198614128.001.0001/odnb-9780198614128-e-29410, accessed 4 December 2019.

14 Arthur H. Cash, *John Wilkes: the scandalous father of civil liberty* (London & New Haven, CT, 2006).
15 Joseph Moxon, *Mechanick exercises: or the doctrine of handy-works applied to the art of printing* (London, 1683), 16–17.
16 P. E. Raynor, 'Printing for amateurs', *Printing Historical Society Journal* 23, 1994, 5–76.
17 Raynor, 'Printing for amateurs'.
18 James Moran, *Printing presses: history and development from the fifteenth century to modern times* (London, 1972).
19 Moran, *Printing presses*.
20 A process by which an image is incised into a surface of a zinc or copper plate and the incised line or sunken area holds the ink.
21 Jean Adhemar, *Graphic art of the eighteenth century* (London, 1964), 43, 106, 108, 113.
22 Margaret Trouncer, *The Pompadour* (London, 1937), 218.
23 Perrin Stein, Marie-Anne Dupuy-Vachey, Eunice Williams and Kelsey Brosnan, *Fragonard: drawing triumphant* (London & New Haven, CT, 2016).
24 Moxon, *Mechanick exercises*, lii.
25 Jabez Francis, *Printing at home: with full instructions of amateurs* (Rochford, 1870).
26 Charles Holtzapffel, *Printing apparatus for the use of amateurs: containing full and practical instructions for the use of Cowper's parlour printing press* (London, 1846).
27 David Garden Berri, *The art of printing* (London, 1864).
28 Francis, *Printing at home*; *How to print* (London, 1875); P. E. Raynor, *Printing for amateurs: a practical guide to the art of printing, illustrated* (London, 1876).
29 Lyndall Gordon, 'Woolf [née Stephen] (Adeline) Virginia (1882–1941), writer and publisher', *Oxford dictionary of national biography* (Oxford, 2004). Online, https://0-www-oxforddnb-com.catalogue.wellcomelibrary.org/view/10.1093/ref:odnb/9780198614128.001.0001/odnb-9780198614128-e-37018, accessed 18 January 2021.
30 S. P. Rosenbaum, 'Woolf, Leonard Sidney (1880–1969), author and publisher', *Oxford dictionary of national biography* (Oxford, 2004). Online, https://0-www-oxforddnb-com.catalogue.wellcomelibrary.org/view/10.1093/ref:odnb/9780198614128.001.0001/odnb-9780198614128-e-37019, accessed 18 January 2021.
31 *Kew Gardens* was first published privately in 1919 by the Woolfs at the Hogarth Press, then more widely in 1921 in the collection *Monday or Tuesday*, and subsequently in the posthumous collection *A haunted house* (1944).
32 Robert Graves, *Good-bye to all that* (London, 1960).
33 Richard Perceval Graves, 'Graves, Robert von Ranke (1895–1985), poet and novelist', *Oxford dictionary of national biography* (Oxford, 2010). Online, https://0-www-oxforddnb-com.catalogue.wellcomelibrary.org/view/10.1093/ref:odnb/9780198614128.001.0001/odnb-9780198614128-e-31166, accessed 18 January 2021.
34 Thomas Graves, 'Robert Graves as printer', in *Bartkowiaks forum book art* (Hamburg, 2005/6) 62–88.
35 Elizabeth Friedmann, *A mannered grace: the life of Laura (Riding) Jackson* (Persea Books, New York, 2005).
36 Laura Riding, *Love as love: death as death* (London, 1928).

37 A. E. Musson, *The Typographical Association, origins and history up to 1949* (Oxford, 1954).
38 David King Dunaway, 'Huxley, Aldous Leonard (1894–1963), writer', *Oxford dictionary of national biography* (Oxford, 2011). Online, https://0-www-oxford dnb-com.catalogue.wellcomelibrary.org/view/10.1093/ref:odnb/978019861 4128.001.0001/odnb-9780198614128-e-34082, accessed 18 January 2021.
39 Aldous Huxley, 'Introduction', in O. Simon & J. Rodenberg (eds) *Printing of today* (London, 1928).
40 Mosley, 'The press in the parlour'.
41 Old Bailey Proceedings Online, www.oldbaileyonline.org, version 8.0, 11 January 2021, August 1683, trial of John Culefant (t16830829-14).
42 Old Bailey Proceedings Online, www.oldbaileyonline.org, version 8.0, 11 January 2021, September 1690, trial of John Lowthorp (t16900903-51).
43 1 Mark = 13*s* 4*d.*
44 Old Bailey Proceedings Online, www.oldbaileyonline.org, version 8.0, 14 January 2021, July 1675, trial of pretended Printer (t16750707-9).
45 Bank of England, 'Counterfeit and imitation notes'. Online, https://www.ban kofengland.co.uk/museum/online-collections/banknotes/counterfeit-and-imitat ion-notes, accessed 18 January 2021.
46 Caroline Archer, 'Despite digital growth the promissory note persists', *Print Week*. Online, https://www.printweek.com/features/article/despite-digital-g rowth-the-promissory-note-persists, accessed 18 January 2021.
47 *Bell's weekly messenger* (London, 1789).
48 J. E. Hall Williams, 'The Ladies' Directory and criminal conspiracy: the judge as custos morum', *The Modern Law Review* 24, 1961, v, 626–631. Online, www .jstor.org/stable/1092876, accessed 14 January 2021.
49 Michael Barber, 'Neville, Richard Clive (1941–2016), writer, editor, and provocateur', *Oxford dictionary of national biography* (Oxford, 2020). Online, https://0-www-oxforddnb-com.catalogue.wellcomelibrary.org/view/10.1093/ ref:odnb/9780198614128.001.0001/odnb-9780198614128-e-112026, accessed 18 January 2021.
50 Caroline Archer, *Tart cards: London's illicit advertising art* (New York, 2003).
51 Gilbert & George. Online, http://www.gilbertandgeorge.co.uk, accessed 9 February 2021.

2 Orlando Erasto Portela

Relations Between the Creative Process and Letterpress Printing Methods of an (Almost) Unknown Designer from the Mid-Twentieth Century

Nuno Coelho

Introduction

This chapter describes how letterpress as a communication medium has been used to convey "Portugality", a concept that combines both modernist (the use of simple and geometric shapes, and plain colours) and traditional (rural and popular motifs) principles. Focusing on the work of Orlando Erasto Portela, and on his personal and professional life, this chapter begins by analysing his influences and describing his creative process; it will further contextualise his work under the Estado Novo and will then undertake an in-detail analysis of a wide sample of labels and packages for consumer products, based on the major cultural, historical, and social themes chosen to illustrate them and also on the technical constraints of letterpress printing methods.

The chosen sample was produced between the late 1940s and the early 1960s for the Confiança soap and perfume factory, and its choice, as a case study for this chapter, is justified by the fact that Erasto was involved in the process of setting up the in-house letterpress workshop at the factory premises, in 1950, as part of a series of major investments in the industrial park and the expansion of this producer based in Braga. Erasto also devoted most of his creations to Confiança. His work reflects the ideology for the "Campaign of Good Taste", commissioned by the Estado Novo regime, that reveals the direct influence of Portuguese cultural heritage on the graphic design of consumer products.

Erasto's Life and Work

Orlando Erasto Portela was born in Porto, Portugal, in 1930. Self-taught from an early age and without any formal artistic training, he began his professional

DOI: 10.4324/9781003173113-4

life as an illustrator at around ten years of age, working at the Litografia Pátria (Pátria Letterpress Workshop) in Porto. It was here that Erasto, the name by which he then signed his work, began to design graphic motifs for packaging and product labels for a range of industries, predominantly located in northern Portugal, including Ach. Brito, Confiança, and many others. His work often extended to the choice of oral brand names (words) whose typography he developed in a personalised manner, giving it a distinctive character in its graphic appearance, in combination with the chosen motifs.

Around 1954, Erasto moved to Braga to work at the then recently opened Litografia Minho (Minho Letterpress Workshop). Twelve years later he moved to Guimarães to work at the Competidora de Representações, a company which printed labels. In 1970, he started working at Plásticos Xavier, also based in Guimarães. He retired in the early 1990s and moved back to Porto. Although he continued to work as an independent illustrator, the work he carried out after his retirement was timely.

Before the proliferation of internet use, Erasto collected numerous clippings with photographs taken from newspapers and magazines, which he organised by themes in archive folders ("faces", "hands", "birds", "fish", among many others) and which served as useful material for his graphic creations. Throughout his life he travelled mostly through Spain and the Netherlands, but his greatest artistic influence was the cinema, which he eagerly watched on an almost daily basis. He died in 2001, in Porto, at the age of 71.

Erasto's Work for Confiança

While working at Litografia Pátria, Erasto started to design labels for Confiança, one of the best and oldest examples of Portuguese custom-brand lithographic prints in Portugal that, since its foundation in 1894, has taken special care in the presentation of its products.[1] Its packaging and label portfolio present a wide range of themes for a set of cosmetics and personal hygiene consumer products. It can therefore easily be said that the dynamism and creativity implemented by Erasto in the packaging and labels for Confiança are good examples of the best graphic design that was carried out in Portugal, spanning several decades in the middle of the twentieth century. Erasto's designs were innovative not only for their exceptional technical quality but also for his aesthetic sense in solving the problems raised by the commercial message to be conveyed. His work became a symbol of a certain sense of modernity and sophistication in a country that still saw itself as being rural and conservative, as well as distant, both geographically and culturally, from the rest of Europe.

In 1950, Confiança set up its in-house letterpress workshop, for which various printing, cutting, and creasing machines were purchased over a period of two years. The existing Heidelberg Cylinder Press was the third of its kind to arrive in Portugal.² Two Heidelberg Platen Presses were also acquired. Confiança also acquired several collections of movable types, blades, strips, and cliches, all of which were distributed in 61 type cases, purchased from foreign foundries, in particular from the Fundición Tipográfica Nacional, in Spain, and Lettergieterij, in the Netherlands. Confiança also purchased a guillotine machine, two shear presses, a dry relief printer, a hand-held engraving and cutting press, and a gilding machine. The letterpress workshop was completed with a carton section consisting of six other machines for different purposes.

It should be noted that, until 1950, Confiança only had a single manual press, thus demonstrating the company's major investment in the installation of its own letterpress workshop. When completed, three printmakers were employed to work simultaneously there, to cater to Confiança's label production needs. At this letterpress workshop, numerous graphic works developed by Erasto, resulting in the production of numerous zinc engraving plates (etching, for custom designs), were produced in large-scale print runs. Many of his designs can still be found on sale in shops today. Before analysing a sample of Erasto's designs developed for Confiança and the technical features and recurrent themes that he addressed, this chapter will first contextualise his work under the Estado Novo.

The Estado Novo and António Ferro's "Campanha do Bom Gosto"

The harmful effects of the Great Depression irreversibly changed the course of history worldwide, paving the way for the implementation and consolidation of dictatorial regimes at the turn of the 1920s. In Portugal, the Military Dictatorship that was installed in 1926 paved the way for the creation of the Estado Novo (New State) enshrined in the 1933 Constitution. The regime persisted until 1974, resulting in the longest dictatorship in Europe.

Under the auspices of the new regime, measures of isolationism and protectionism were taken in the economy, while in the field of culture the outlines of "Lusitanism"³ and "Portugality" were defined, which involved replacing the image of the "real" country with one whose past and future were idealised according to the Estado Novo's patriotic-clerical mythology (de Almeida, 2009, p. 65). The regime's ideological orientation was transmitted by iconographic and symbolic devices present in the arts and design developed during this time. Despite the late institutionalisation of design in Portugal (de Almeida, 2009), the Estado Novo became aware of its importance by including this discipline, at the time called "applied art", in the "Campanha do Bom Gosto" ("Campaign of Good Taste"). This term was coined in 1941 by the journalist and writer, António Ferro, who oversaw the propaganda and cultural policy of the Estado Novo.

This campaign provided a guide of good practices to raise the standards of artistic creation, particularly interested in the arts, decoration, graphic arts, and advertising according to nationalist ideals, valuing popular traditions and folk manifestations (Santos, 2003, p. 24). Its goal was the defence and promotion of national historical-ethnographic heritage through a cultural contribution of re-inventing national identities and memories, through the combination of myths, fantasies, and historical truths. The "good taste" that was programmed and imposed by the regime transversely permeated all the applied arts, including the design of packaging for everyday consumer products. This ideological alignment of the brand design was a form, albeit symbolic, for the Estado Novo to enter the private sphere of Portuguese people, i.e. in their own homes.

Under the Estado Novo, graphics were strongly influenced by the new trends of geometric expressionism that were being imported essentially from Germany, but also with French influences, combining modernism (functional and synthetic compositions) with conservatism (bucolic and traditionalist motifs). The combination of these two apparently antagonistic characteristics, engineered by Ferro, was influenced by the fact that he was part of the modernist movement in Portugal. Ferro's removal from his leading role in 1949 dictated the progressive abandonment of traditionalist themes in the Estado Novo's cultural policy. "Rural themes [were then] seconded in favour of others closer to the imaginary of urbanised populations" (Fragoso, 2012, pp. 118–119).[4]

Semiotic Analysis of a Sample of Graphic Motifs Developed by Erasto

Throughout his life, Erasto worked anonymously either in the places where he worked or as an independent graphic designer. He did not sign any of his designs. His authorship was linked to a wide sample of labels produced by Confiança by conducting interviews with former workers at this factory, including one former printmaker, and one of his descendants (Coelho, 2013; Coelho, 2017). Erasto never worked for the state. However, his work widely reflects Ferro's guidelines of the "Campanha do Bom Gosto", as this section will now demonstrate. A taxonomy of themes was developed from an analysis of a sample of labels whose authorship was attributed to him.

Human Figure

Despite the fact that the human figure is the theme with the highest number of cases, most of it appears to be in relation to others. Examples are the motifs developed for the soap labels "Tricana" (a traditional style of women's clothing), "Ceifeira" (a female reaper from southern Portugal), "Algarvia" ("Woman from the Algarve"), among many others, in which the figurative representation of human presence denotes typical activities and folk traditions (Figure 2.1). It is, therefore, a visual language in accordance with the spirit of the Estado Novo.

A smaller number of labels show the female figure as synonymous with sophistication and beauty and some adopted Portuguese feminine given names as brand designations. The male figure appears in literal illustrations that represent it in daily hygiene care activities, such as the various labels for shaving powder that illustrate a man shaving his beard. Children appear in motifs that can be interpreted as synonymous with happiness and innocence, such as the labels for the product range "Banho do Bebé" ("Baby Bath"). In a unique case, a child is pictured with his mother, in a motif that suggests maternal affection.

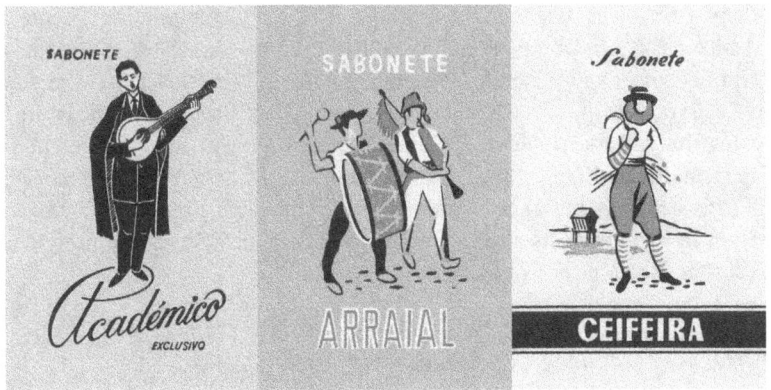

Figure 2.1 Three Labels of Soaps for the Brand Académico, Featuring an Illustration of a Male Student from the University of Coimbra Singing to Fado While Playing a Portuguese Guitar; Arraial, Featuring an Illustration of Two Men in a Folk Dress Playing Drums and Bagpipes; and Ceifeira, Featuring an Illustration of a Female Reaper Holding a Scythe, and a Wheat Branch.

24 *Nuno Coelho*

Flowers, Nature, and Landscapes

As expected, one of the most recurring themes is related to elements from nature and natural places, wherein flowers were the most common element. This fact is easily explained by the direct relationship between the aroma of flowers and that of soaps, as is the case of products with aromas of lavender, rose, carnation, violet and jasmine. Although, in some cases, the brand name does not adopt the name of the flower from which it uses its aroma, flowers, and other plant motifs appear as an illustrative adornment for many labels. Floral motifs have also never ceased to be largely associated with femininity, wherein women are the preferred target audience of the cosmetic industry.

International References

In terms of international references, several cases related to foreign countries and languages were identified. France is the country with the highest number of associations and almost all references refer to its capital, such as the labels for the soaps "Paris", "Rivoli", "Flores de Paris" ("Paris Flowers"), "Rosas de Paris" ("Paris Roses"), and others. In turn, the French language appears in brand names such as "Bon Jour" and others. Spain is the country with the second-highest number of entries, such as the labels for "Espanhola" ("Spanish Woman"), "Sevilhano" ("Man from Seville"), and others. Castilian is also used in a few brand names such as "La Goya", and others. Brazil was related to the labels "Baião" (a Brazilian musical genre), "Amazona" ("Amazon Woman"), and "Rio". Egypt was related to the labels "Nilo" ("Nile") and "Camelo" ("Camel"), whose illustration shows a camel by the Pyramids of Giza. Other countries were identified, such as the United States, Italy, Turkey, Mexico, Chile, Scotland, Argentina, Monaco, Iraq, Japan, India, and Germany. From the analysis of international references, there is a strong presence of motifs associated with France, a reference nation in relation to its strong cosmetic industry, and Spain, the preferred export destination for Confiança.

Portuguese Mainland Geo-Ethnographic References

Regarding Portuguese mainland[5] geo-ethnographic references, the representation of typical, folk, and popular activities was verified. This was a widely recurring theme from the 1940s onwards, resulting from the alliance of modern and traditional concepts within the scope of Ferro's cultural policies. Illustrations picturing festivities, pilgrimages, and festivals, as well as agricultural activities, are common. Also, symbolic locations illustrating the concept of "Portugality" were widely adopted, such as "Nazaré" (a Portuguese traditional fishing town), "Rosas da Madeira" ("Madeira Island's Roses"), "Açores" ("Azores Islands"), and many others. Through analysis of this theme, it was verified the logic of valorisation of the national heritage in a language that was in line with the rediscovery of the typical and folk Portuguese roots.

National Symbols and Historical Figures and Events

In the analysis of this theme, the motifs inspired by national-patriotic topics are highlighted, such as the labels for "Caravella" ("Caravel"), "Castelo" ("Castle"), "Cavaleiros" ("Horsemen"), "Conquistador" ("Conqueror"), "Templários" ("Templars"), and others picturing known castles and other national monuments. Historical figures and events, such as battles, are also present. Like the previous theme, this one also refers to questions related to the historical collective identity.

Architecture

With regard to architectural elements, these appear to be primarily subordinated in relation to other themes, namely to those included in the previous theme. Closer references to the concepts of development and progress can be seen through the labels for "Alvalade" (a Lisbon neighbourhood), whose illustration represents multi-storey buildings at the new avenues that were built in the Portuguese capital in the 1940s, and others illustrating major engineering works developed under the Estado Novo. Analysis of this theme reveals an evident celebration of major public infrastructure investments made by the political regime.

Animals

In relation to animals, there are literal cases of representation such as the choice of motifs and brand names for "Mariposa" ("Butterfly"), "Melro" ("Blackbird"), and "Pinto" ("Chick", also a common Portuguese surname). In other cases, there was no clear reason for choosing animal motifs, such as the ones featuring a squirrel, a mink, or a pair of doves. Other animals were found, although subordinated to other themes, such as the rattlesnake pictured on the label for "Africano" ("African"), and others, which were linked to colonial references. Confiança also developed cleaning products for pets, such as "Gá-Ti-Cão" ("Ca-Tan-Dog") featuring a cat and a dog. Analysis of this theme reveals that its symbolic use is more ambiguous than in the cases analysed previously.

26 *Nuno Coelho*

Colonial References

In the analysis of associations with the Portuguese Empire, product labels were observed with motifs related to the former Portuguese colonies. Among the identified cases, the representation of native populations and their cultural manifestations was found, as well as exotic motifs. Examples are the labels for "Morna" (a Cape Verdean musical genre), "Merengue" and "Mambo" (both Angolan musical genres). When illustrations representing local inhabitants were used, these appeared in stigmatised representations, showing no traces of Western "civility". This representation was in line with the regime's ideology, which, by perpetuating stereotypes, intended to maintain the feeling of the coloniser's superiority and, consequently, the hegemony of the Empire. Among colonial references, Angola occupied a prominent place, considered the "crown jewel" of the Portuguese Empire, as the largest and richest Portuguese colony at that time.

Music and Dance

In this category there is a predominance of themes related to typical Portuguese manifestations. Examples are the labels for "Académico", featuring a student from the University of Coimbra singing Fado while playing a Portuguese guitar, "Vira do Minho" (a folk dance from northern Portugal), and others. Musical genres from the former colonies and foreign countries were also represented, some already mentioned in previous categories. References to musical genres considered to be more erudite were lesser present, such as the ones for "Serenata" ("Serenade"), "Ballet", and "Melodia" ("Melody"), the latter featuring a violin and two brass instruments.

Sport

In this category, football is by far the most represented sport. The names of famous football players were chosen for brand names, such as "Pelé". Labels were also designed for the leading Portuguese football clubs, such as those produced for Benfica, FC Porto, and Sporting. The label for "Everest", whose illustration represents a mountain climber, is the only under this theme that is not related to football, a sporting activity that is considered to have been instrumentalised by the Estado Novo as a tool for national unity.

Religion

In this category, most of the motifs are related to religious buildings, such as the ones representing saints and façades of churches. The relationship between the Catholic Church and the State was restored during the Military Dictatorship (1926–1933) after approval of their separation in the First Republic (1910–1926), through the adoption of a series of anti-clerical measures. The major influence of the Church during the Portuguese dictatorship may explain the use of religious-inspired labels.

Geometric and Abstract

In addition to the previous themes, a shorter number of labels were identified, whose compositions were purely geometric and abstract. In the absence of figurative elements, the hypothesis of formulating considerations about their possible meaning was obliterated.

Relations Between Creative Process and Letterpress Printing Methods

The analysis of a sample of Erasto's work for Confiança aimed to achieve a fuller understanding of designers as creators of images in the process of building a genuinely Portuguese style, combining both modern and traditional concepts. The observed use of simple and geometric shapes and plain flat colours, characteristics of Erasto's visual lexicon, was not only in line with Ferro's idealised "Campaign of Good Taste", but were also dictated by the technical possibilities and constraints of the letterpress printing process.

In the vast majority of cases, Erasto downsized the number of colours per label to three or four for the purpose of both communication (combining and matching colours accurately) and budget (spending control) efficiency. However, cases of labels featuring five or even six colours were observed. This choice resulted in a more expensive production of these labels but also meant that the corresponding results were graphically more dynamic, possibly representing one-off investments by Confiança in some of its brands.

Throughout the entire chosen sample, the wide use of plain flat colours on the motifs and backgrounds of the labels is justified by the letterpress printing methods, where ink is actually pressed onto the paper using custom-designed zinc engraving plates (one plate per each colour, one colour at a time). This technical constraint of plain flat colours that had to be used was not considered to be a problem since it followed modernist aesthetics.

Conclusion

It is largely assumed that the genesis of graphic design, as an autonomous discipline, was largely a consequence of the Industrial Revolution. The autonomy of this discipline was consolidated during the twentieth century, not only as a result of this industrial progress but also of a set of political, economic, social, cultural, and artistic transformations. If societies face profound transformations over time, so does design. This way, it can easily be said that a certain visual hegemony is a historical reflection, a mirror, of its contemporary society. History, events, and policies conducted over the twentieth century directly influenced and shaped the visual universe idealised by designers. In turn, the design also helped to influence and shape societies. Bearing this in mind, design can be understood as a cultural product, in other words just "as social practices generate images, images generate social practices" (Ciarlo, 2011, p. 3). Thus, using Erasto's work for Confiança as a case study, this chapter demonstrates the direct influence of Portuguese cultural heritage on the graphic design of consumer products (and vice-versa) whose labels were produced by letterpress printing methods.

Notes

1 The company remains active today, so its activity spans the entire 20th century.
2 The first was bought by Diário de Notícias daily newspaper, in Lisbon, and the second by O Comércio do Porto daily newspaper, in Porto. The exact dates are not known.
3 Lusitania was the name given by the Roman Empire to the region where Portugal was subsequently formed.
4 However, we would have to wait for the 1960s to finally experience the erosion of the political regime, and of the intrinsic link between political power and artistic creation in Portugal. The dictatorship was finally ousted by a military-led revolution in 1974.
5 Under the Estado Novo, Portugal maintained its control over several colonies in Africa and Asia. The term "mainland" here refers to its European territory, which corresponds to present-day Portugal.

References

de Almeida, Victor (2009). *O design em Portugal, um tempo e um modo: a institucionalização do design português entre 1959–1974* (Ph.D. thesis in Design). Lisbon: Universidade de Lisboa. Retrieved from: http://hdl.handle.net/10451/2485.
Ciarlo, David (2011). *Advertising Empire – Race and Visual Culture in Imperial Germany*. London: Harvard University Press.
Coelho, Nuno (2013). *O Design de embalagem em Portugal no século XX – Do funcional ao simbólico – O estudo de caso da Saboaria e Perfumaria Confiança* (Ph.D. thesis in Contemporary Art). Coimbra: Universidade de Coimbra. Retrieved from: http://hdl.handle.net/10316/23803.

Coelho, Nuno (2017). *Uma história de Confiança: A indústria da saboaria e perfumaria no século XX português*. Lisbon: Tinta-da-china.

Fragoso, Margarida (2012). *Design Gráfico em Portugal – Formas e Expressões da Cultura Visual do Século XX*. Lisbon: Livros Horizonte.

Santos, Rui Afonso (2003). *Cadeiras Contemporâneas Portuguesas*. Alfragide: ASA.

3 *The Mark on the Wall*

Ane Thon Knutsen

Introduction

This chapter presents a project that emerged from my interest in hybrid letterpress practice and the attempt to define one's place in history, as a female self-taught printer from the other side of the digital revolution.

Reflecting on Virginia Woolf's essay, *A Room of One's Own,* helped me clarify the crucial role played by material conditions for artistic practice.

This case study consists of research into and through Virginia Woolf's short story, *The Mark on the Wall*, which she wrote while she taught herself to typeset. She acknowledged the importance of the printing press in her road to artistic freedom. Moving along the outer lines of the current professional graphic design activity to discuss and challenge the definitions of both the profession and the craft's place and role, both historically and today, the project has resulted in a number of works that can be placed between technical and methodological experiments, results and reflection. In this research I explain why I consider that typography was a large (yet highly underestimated) part of Virginia Woolf's work as an author.

Case Study

This research sprang from my interest in printed media in a digital age, focusing on artistic work. [Re]searching into tactility in printed matter, I immersed myself in the Norwegian printing industry and sought out what remains of original environments that still have expertise in traditional letterpress in order to embody some of their knowledge. I typeset various texts by other authors, but after several weeks of trial and error, I began to become increasingly annoyed by the uneconomic manner in which the texts were written – not with the typecase in mind, but as word documents. Typesetting began to change how I read and experienced text.

Typesetting every word involves a manual job that takes up space and time. One must live with the words as a material element. I became very picky about my own writing. Everything superfluous had to go in order to achieve a good balance between long and short words. When I was composing, I edited the text whenever the words did not make up a nice line, or to avoid rivers or hyphens. As I worked, day after day, I felt that my body was automating the process; I began to think about my heritage. As a female, self-taught printer, I noticed differences in backgrounds and professional viewpoints. Maybe this originates from a completely different place from the industry? Maybe the industrial legacy isn't mine to appropriate? Working in museums and shared workshops, my work was also influenced by being an artist in residence; I could not concentrate and reflect on the act of typesetting for longer periods of time.

At this point I discovered the famous essay *A Room of One's Own*[1] (1929) by Virginia Woolf (1882–1941).

In this text Woolf addresses the causes for women's intellectual and material poverty across the ages and suggests the importance of having a room of one's own and a small steady income as a solution for intellectual development. In an essay that is often viewed in the context of her text, *Three Guineas*[2] (1938), Virginia Woolf attacks the elite – professors, politicians and the clergy – and blames the patriarchy for all the miseries in the world. She explicitly encourages women to obtain printing presses. At the time the text was received with intense criticism and she was accused of being hysterical and mad. But the most interesting fact is that she was able to publish the essay: because she owned a printing press, and with that she had the creative freedom and opportunity to publish whatever she wanted, at a time when women had only just secured the right to vote in England.

Virginia Woolf's *A Room of One's Own* put into words things that I was struggling with. I saw that the structural challenges that women have faced since the dawn of time still apply. And I realised that a workshop that could be locked from the inside is required for uninterrupted intellectual development. Learning that Woolf was a self-taught typesetter, bookbinder and publisher, fuelled my own personal obsession with Virginia Woolf and The Hogarth Press.

The Hogarth Press

Leonard and Virginia Woolf purchased a printing press in March 1917.[3] This was initially viewed primarily as a hobby, but they soon realised that it had greater potential. Leonard – due to his trembling hands – printed and Virginia composed and dissed type, folded and bound books.

Their very first publication was *Two Stories* (1917),⁴ which had a print run of 150 copies. The pamphlet consists of eight sections, plus covers, with a total of 32 pages, which took them three months to complete. It is printed on thin, semi-coated paper, and set in 10-point Caslon Old Face. *Three Jews* by Leonard Woolf had 14 pages, *The Mark on the Wall* by Virginia Woolf had 12. In addition, there is a title page, a table of contents and four illustrations (woodcuts) by Dora Carrington. The British Library's version has a cover of blue Japanese paper. The pamphlet is stitched with blue cotton thread, through three holes. The printing press they used was a small hand press, which could print one page (half a spread) at a time. The amount of type was limited, so Virginia could compose a maximum of two to three pages before she started to run out of letters. Once the pages were printed, she had to put every letter and every space back before composing the following pages.

Virginia soon realised that this technology gave her the power to manifest her thoughts into a physical format. *The Mark on the Wall* was the first taste of freedom that made her a writer, whose lines of thought stretched all the way into the canon. She herself clarified the significance of The Hogarth Press for her:

> How my handwriting goes down hill! Another sacrifice to The Hogarth Press. Yet what I owe The Hogarth Press is barely paid by the whole of my handwriting. Haven't I just written to Herbert Fisher refusing to do a book for the Home University Series on Post-Victorian? – knowing that I can write a book, a better book, a book of my own bat, for the press if I wish! To think of being battened down in the hold of those University Dons fairly making my blood run cold. Yet I am the only woman in England free to write what I like. The others must be thinking of series and editors.⁵
>
> (Virginia Woolf, *The Diary of Virginia Woolf 3*, 1977–82, pp. 42–43)

A Printing Press of One's Own

Before I became a mother, I worked whenever I was able to be alone in the workshops. But this was no longer possible. Interruptions and disturbances from others were not compatible with composing and my need for profound concentration. After learning about The Hogarth Press, I understood what I needed.

We rebuilt half of our basement into a letterpress workshop, and on March 23, 2017, the date that marked a hundred years after Woolf bought her printing press, I had my own.

A few days after completing the essay, *A Printing Press of One's Own*, I came across an invitation to exhibit printed works commemorating the centenary of Virginia Woolf and The Hogarth Press.[6] In June I travelled to a conference with Woolf-experts from around the world. At this point I thought this might be the end of my Woolf track. Maybe I would find all the answers and be able to return to tactility in printed matter. I still thought that objective answers were possible that could be provided by theory.

I gained valuable insight and met interesting and knowledgeable people. However, most of the lectures came from literary science, and not from the typecase, where my questions had arisen. My questions became increasingly intriguing – I began to see potential in my own project. The questions arising from the typecase could at best have the opportunity to illuminate certain areas that literary science cannot reach. Thinking-doing and writing-composing cannot live solely in the language; they live just as much in the body. I also realised that an objective truth wasn't what really interested me. What I wanted to achieve was a proximity zone to the book as material, the meta-physical and physical entity, and to read the text also through materials. For example, it may resemble the way that Maurice Merelau-Ponty in *The World of Perception*[7] thinks we should understand honey. There is no single objective property that defines or *is* honey. We have to understand it based on how its various different properties speak to our senses through taste, consistency, colour, among others, which all vary from jar to jar – but they are all honey, based on a group of classifications that cannot be anything but honey.

The Mark on the Wall

I decided to delve deep into *The Mark on the Wall*, which Woolf wrote while she was teaching herself letterpress. Not intending to write a literary analysis – but to make artistic interpretations and adaptations of what aroused some sort of recognition. The short story is an experiment using the form known as "stream of consciousness" and it rebels against those who seek to rationalise, concretise, regulate into frameworks that govern and control. It fights against generalisations, against the "boring", which briefly defines what something is.

The Mark on the Wall is set in a solid interior, a room that encloses the subject, where her train of thoughts repeatedly departs from and returns to the mark on the wall and changes in line with the subject's imagination. The subject in the text does not seek a single answer or direction. She does not want to concretise; she opposes reality and dreams and lingers in the freedom of thought, which travels from the mark on the wall, as if everything exists behind/in/through the wall. Nothing is solid, least of all the wall. A wall is both inside and out: part of our personal sphere, and part of the rest of the world. Virginia Woolf often uses the body as a metaphor, describing her own writing process as a mixture of wandering thoughts and buildings. Rooms that enclose or close out.

What happens to the text when the author writes the book and also controls all its constituent parts? Many commentators believe that *The Mark on the Wall* refers to the book. The short story is a product of an author who is profoundly involved in the book's physical production, and we can choose to read the text in dialogue with the creation of *Two Stories*. Although *The Mark on the Wall* is not considered to be important in the broad outlines of Woolf's writing, I think it offers a key. Woolf included clear references to composing type in her essay *How Should One Read a Book?* (1926):[8]

> Try to understand what a writer is doing. Think of a book as a very dangerous and exciting game, which it takes two to play at. Books are not turned out of moulds like bricks. Books are made of tiny little words, which a writer shapes, often with great difficulty, into sentences of different lengths, placing one on top of another, never taking his eye off them, sometimes building them quite quickly, at other times knocking them down in despair, and beginning all over again.[9]
>
> (H. Lee, 1996, p.368)

Adaptations

In 2017, I began making adaptations of *The Mark on the Wall*. I presented two of them, which were important since they formed the conclusion presented as my practice-based PhD at the Oslo National Academy of the Arts in 2019.

28 Colours

For some weeks I left words as form and worked only on the colours described in the story. Virginia Woolf had an ambition to try and "paint in prose", inspired by, among others, her sister and artist Vanessa Bell (1879–1961) and the painter Paul Cézanne (1839–1906). *The Mark on the Wall* is clearly an experiment in that direction. I wanted to explore stream of consciousness as a method and combine it with my subjective perceptions of the correct colours. When my train of thought stopped at a thought that matched the colour that I saw, I printed a rectangle in the same size as *Two Stories* with that colour. These were my own interpretations, rather than a search for Virginia Woolf's colours. I had taken her advice from *The Mark on the Wall* seriously and viewed my ownership of the essay as a tool.

> nothing is known, nothing is certain (…) And what is Knowledge? (…) Think calmly, spaciously without any sense of hostility or obstacle.[10]

Punctum

10 full stops using 10 different fonts, in 1,296 points, were printed black by photopolymer plates on white A2 sheets. The prints are riddles to test whether people can place the typeface solely on the basis of the shape and placement of a full stop on a sheet. But the intention was layered; because when trying to make out the font, you are looking at a mark on the wall, and you will soon start to think about something else entirely.

For a type composer, the full stop has a kind of double role. When the body has automated the process, one's own thoughts start to wander beyond the text at hand. When you get to a full stop, you return to the manuscript and check the next sentence and your thoughts stop. The fact that the full stop and the mark on the wall are related to each other is obvious and a quite common speculation.

> The mark was a small round mark, black upon the white wall, about six or seven inches above the mantlepiece.
> (Woolf, 1917, p. 20)[11]

> Still, there's no harm in putting a full stop to one's disagreeable thoughts by looking at a mark on the wall.
> (Woolf, 1917, p. 29)[12]

Conclusion

The outcome of this artistic research on Virginia Woolf was presented as a monumental installation at the Kunstnernes Hus in Oslo, in January 2019 (Figure 3.1).

The format/boundaries of this work were the physical relationship between the number of words and the size of paper, the press, the type and the room. The room is the format, the room is the text and the text is the room, which *The Mark on the Wall* reflects upon.

I CNC milled out a set of Carol Twombly's Adobe Caslon Pro, bold, upper case, in 14-point Cicero, referencing Caslon Old Face that was used by The Hogarth Press. This set of type was used to print the entire *The Mark*

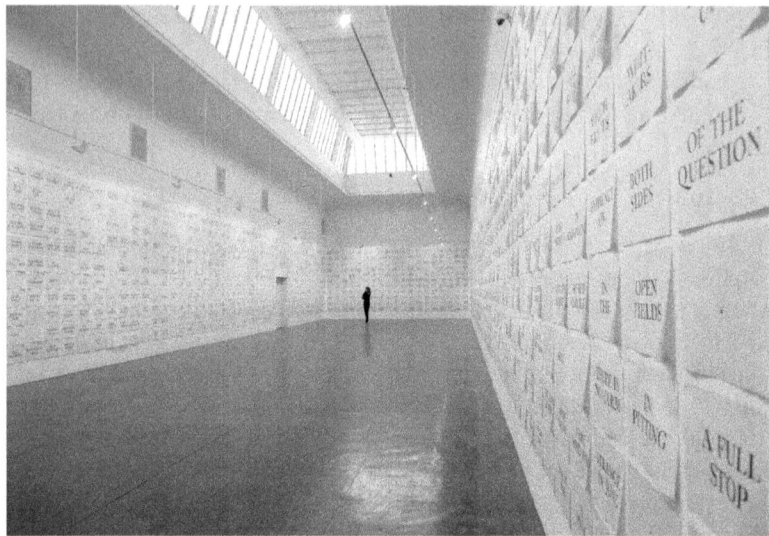

Figure 3.1 1837 Letterpress Prints on Newsprint That Make Up the Entire Short Story *The Mark on the Wall*, Written and Printed by Virginia Woolf. Kunstnernes Hus.

on the Wall, with 1–5 words on each sheet, making up 1837 A3 sheets of newsprint. In addition, there is a timelapse video of the three months of intensive printing and an audiobook with my reflections during the production. I moved the proximity zone from a small pamphlet into a huge, public space. All prints were later disassembled and bound together as a single monumental book. I have changed several words in this story for typographic reasons, to avoid hyphens, as I claim Woolf did while struggling in front of the typecase, in the spring of 1917.

The aim of this work was to illustrate composing type, by flipping the entire relationship between composing and reading in relation to the body: from something intimate and tangible, to something that is large and fragmented. This enables readers to physically enter the story and walk around inside it. It was possible to read chronologically or as form and fragments. Each print was an entity and a part of a whole, in the same way as the text proposes numerous narratives and stories within stories. But it also concludes that writing, for Virginia Woolf, especially during the production of *Two Stories* was a site-specific endeavour, where the physical demands of composing type and printing might have had the upper hand on her mind in the last edit. The installation aimed to emphasise what is experienced through practising typesetting, where typography exists in the space between fantasy and reality, between thought and speech, subject and object, word and image. The type compositors were trained in form, line breaks, hyphens, composition – the work of the hand. The content of the text was not their business. It was the work of the author and the editor – the work of the mind. I am focusing on Woolf's middle position. She had both literary and typographic knowledge. The hand and the mind. Through my own practice and in the search for explicit reflections on the process of typesetting, I am left with a collection of fragments that indicate that Virginia Woolf kept on editing and interpreting her own and other writers' work, also typographically. In a letter sent to Vita Sackville-West in 1926, she wrote: "dabbling in wet type, which make my fingers frozen; and setting up the poems of Mrs Manning Sanders, which the more I set them, the less I like"[13] (Woolf, 1975–80, pp. 241). When she composed Hope Mirrlees' *Paris* (1919), they sent proofs back and forth with comments on the typography in relation to the content. For example, she tried to illustrate the Jardin des Tuileries typographically.[14] T.S. Eliot told Woolf in a letter that he preferred her version of *The Waste Land* (1923) over the professionally produced American version. Although she struggled to compose the poem, she understood how Eliot used typography as a literary tool.[15] In the 1927 edition of *Kew Gardens*, Vanessa Bell's illustrations almost break up the text and emphasise the fragmentary form of the short story. The form gives associations to a conversation where the sisters' artforms are graphically intertwined. The materiality of literature, typesetting and the production of the book object influenced the literary work of Virginia Woolf, as two sides of the same coin. *The Mark on the Wall* and how it was first produced and published is crucial to understanding that the printing press was absolutely crucial in the development of her writing and her view of language as something that is spatial and material, as a form of architecture. Typesetting, in more ways than one, created one of the greatest writers of our time.

Notes

1 V. Woolf (2012). *Et eget rom, Tre Guineas.* Oslo: Pax.
2 V. Woolf (2012). *Et eget rom, Tre Guineas.* Oslo: Pax.
3 J.H. Willis (1992). *Leonard and Virginia Woolf as Publishers: The Hogarth Press, 1917–41.* Charlottesville and London: University Press of Virginia; H. Lee (1996). 'The Press' in *Virginia Woolf.* New York: Vintage Books; R. Kennedy (1972). *A Boy at the Hogarth Press.* London: Hesperus Press.
4 V. Woolf, & L. Woolf (1917). *Two Stories.* London: The Hogarth Press.
5 D. Porter (2004). *Virginia Woolf and The Hogarth Press: Riding a Great Horse.* London: Cecil Woolf Publishers.

6. N. Wilson, & C. Battershill (ed.) (2018). *Virginia Woolf and the World of Books.* Clemson: Clemson University Press.
7. M. Merleau-Ponty (2017). *The World of Perception.* New York: State University of New York Press.
8. V. Woolf (1948). *The Common Reader, Second Series.* London: The Hogarth Press.
9. H. Lee (1996) *Virginia Woolf.* New York: Vintage Books.
10. V. Woolf, & L. Woolf (1917). *Two Stories.* London: The Hogarth Press.
11. V. Woolf, & L. Woolf (1917). *Two Stories.* London: The Hogarth Press.
12. V. Woolf, & L. Woolf (1917). *Two Stories.* London: The Hogarth Press.
13. V. Woolf (1975–80). *The Letters of Virginia Woolf,* 6 vols., ed. Nigel Nicolson and Joanne Trautmann. London: The Hogarth Press.
14. M. Beech (2018). *Virginia Woolf and the World of Books*, ed. Nicola Wilson and Claire Battershill, Clemson University Press, pp. 70–75.
15. J.H. Willis (1992). *Leonard and Virginia Woolf as Publishers: The Hogarth Press 1917–41*, London: University Press of Virginia.

Part II
Introduction
Education

This part explores the relationship between letterpress practice and design education. There is a growing interest in hands-on practice in contemporary educational contexts. Facing unique pedagogical challenges, the development of new design aesthetics, new teaching methods and the adaption and fabrication of tools are relevant matters to be discussed.

Different authors, researchers, educators and practitioners share their views and personal experiences in making and teaching letterpress and letterforms, both in academic circles in and professional contexts.

Part II presents the current state of the art and main challenges of letterpress education, advocating for its pedagogic value, that goes beyond the nostalgia of materiality or typographic knowledge towards a "thinking-through-making" design-oriented approach that defines maker-cultures, connecting analogue and digital technologies and their practitioners.

The following chapter further explores the idea of letterpress as an applied thinking-driven practice bound to improve graphic design education. It also addresses the history and challenges of setting up a letterpress workshop inside a design school, and how its workflow and space should be adapted.

The fifth chapter presents the many forms of Super Veloz, a modular type system, created in the late 1930s. Initially designed to work as a flexible tool to print custom-built letterforms, illustrations and ornaments, it evolved into an engaging tool for teaching typography, through its digitalisation. The authors discuss the system's various applications, ranging from screen-based apps to digitally fabricated stamps and stencils used for educational purposes, highlighting its figurative and textual capacity, as well as the modularity that helps explain the basics of letter shapes and type design.

The sixth chapter discusses a research project in post-digital letterpress practice. In the case studied, a Letterpress Print Exchange is undertaken, in which the artworks explore a combination of traditional letterpress with a range of digital manufacturing techniques. The collaboration with a diverse

DOI: 10.4324/9781003173113-6

community of practitioners led to the creation of three categories that describe the phenomenon studied.

The seventh chapter presents three case studies that emerge from one of Portugal's few BA Hons degree courses in communication design that integrates a letterpress workshop in its curricula. The projects address basic methodological and technical skills for future communication designers, as well as the ability to work collectively in an informal and enjoyable environment.

Part II
Education Highlight
Poiesis and Purpose: Lessons in Making

Catherine Dixon

Printing technologies come and go, as new methods override past practices, yet letterpress persists within our educational contexts. In terms of design, the rationale for this fixture has been primarily framed in the context of haptic pedagogy. As Anthony Froshaug recognised, in 1946, handling type offers a benefit for the typographic training of a designer, which bridges the experience of design as specification with the reality of print production.[1] Convinced of its educational potential, Froshaug established an early precedent for design-led letterpress tuition and invited Edward Wright to give evening classes at the Central School from 1952 to 1956. In the post-digital environment, screen-based design for printed outcomes similarly operates as a form of specification with that which David Jury describes as, the 'implicit knowledge gained by handling and moving real things around', which still helps to inform awareness of production.[2] However, as Eric Kindel has noted, contemporary interest in letterpress is also driven by a renewed valuation of the materiality of the print itself and the fact that it provides 'a counterweight to the disembodied digital form of much present-day typography and graphic communication'.[3]

Yet there are dangers in foregrounding materiality in a rationale for maintaining letterpress when design education is facing new challenges. What Meredith Davis has identified as 'the artefact-driven goal of design' is being held to account by critics such as Bridgman, due to its contribution to the 'global machinery of production and consumption' and its failure to respond adequately to the complex and uncertain problems that are currently faced by society.[4] In response, a new pedagogic climate is emerging which favours the strategic design of immaterial services over material products.[5] Letterpress sits here precariously. The practical logic of 'the bottom line' is

DOI: 10.4324/9781003173113-7

often hard to negotiate and it is cheaper to educate a strategic thinker than a materials-based practitioner. Further, exaggerations of materiality and the handmade as evidence of craft have become something of a trope in the field of letterpress, and, as Rafael Cardozo has recognised, the identification of 'imperfections and deviations ... as legitimating characteristics' leads only to the danger of being 'cornered into a position of terminal nostalgia'.[6]

Processual approaches are required to re-evaluate in letterpress the possibilities for a maker-intelligence which combines the material and the conceptual. Such an approach to thinking-through-making or what A. Telier describes as 'situated doing' moves beyond production-centred models.[7] As Martina Margetts explains, 'The plan of a design alters in its doing', or as Robin Fior perhaps best expresses it, 'The secret of *poesis* is in the making'.[8] This is an approach that Daniel Charny argues has been devalued in education, although he considers that it is exactly this kind of applied thinking that constitutes an essential part of our future.[9] It is easy to see why in the emergent maker-cultures which are bridging analogue-digital binaries, exploring hacking and open-source hybridities, and opening out what Ele Carpenter has welcomed as experimental and collaborative spaces for 'finding innovative ways to use, reuse and recycle the technologies and materials that we already have'.[10] As Rose Gridneff and Alexander Cooper have observed, 'Print does not need to be the end result'.[11] In the 2009 exhibition *The changing face of letterpress*, they set out to explore the ways in which letterpress could be a medium for 'igniting process-driven work' and, as such, of transdisciplinary pedagogic value beyond the usual concerns with print-centred knowledge-building or typographic understanding.[12]

Necessary and progressive, this open-boundaried outlook also serves as a reminder of the need to re-evaluate practices from the past, free from the lens of nostalgia, which has done so much to muddy articulations of historical practices. Wright's original design-oriented classes from the 1950s similarly followed a 'cross-category drive' in terms of his intended participants.[13] And, while anchored in material experimentation, Wright was actually more concerned with testing communication and meaning at a much broader level, as Carpenter has elaborated of contemporary making practices, with finding out how things work.[14]

Within contemporary making, then, the craft competences of the industrial heritage of letterpress still have a role to play, not least because there are too few technicians who have an in-depth technical understanding of how many of the machines in our letterpress spaces function. Yet, it is important to also acknowledge the possibilities for new identities to emerge. It is a space that Ane Thon Knutsen has sought to explore, since she realises, in spite of having her technical abilities validated in a trade letterpress qualification, that 'The industrial history is not mine to appropriate', instead of acknowledging that her 'place in history, as a female self-taught printer from the other side of the digital revolution, was in fact another'.[15] Further, any ambition to preserve specialist practice should, I would argue, contribute to a new, and as Neil Cummings describes, 'generous collective intelligence'.[16] This is aggregate knowledge-building of specialism which seeks to enthusiastically receive and not to control, with the intention of overcoming the protective barriers that a sense of specialism, especially one that is threatened, can all-too-quickly establish. Encouragingly, there is evidence of this in the operation of new maker-networks, including letterpress communities, through peer-to-peer skill-sharing and making the process public, often using social media.[17] Digital once again fuses with analogue as online technologies support craft-making and the desire of makers to connect with others through their making. And as Rosy Greenless and Mark Jones have observed, 'the desire to make together in a social context is growing ever stronger'.[18]

The immediacy of access to a printing press and the modest scale of production that letterpress affords has historically enabled printers and designers to engage in local forms of social and political activism. Desmond Jeffery and Robin Fior both identified a potential for political resistance in their use of letterpress during the 1960s and into the 1970s. More recently the Argentinian designer Federico Cimatti has, under the imprint Prensa La Libertad, activated a press for the dissemination of community-focused protest messages. Also in Spain, an economic crisis prompted the Catalan collective L'Automàtica to explore resourceful ways to continue their creative work. They took on a failing letterpress business, keeping the printer on to train them, while also exploring the potential of the press to activate and engage the local community to help redress the dire political context. The idea of utilising letterpress to directly equip a community has also been a goal of Atêlie Acaia, an educational initiative in São Paulo that invested in a second-hand printing press for a group of teenagers living in the direst of circumstances. (Figure P2.1 shows retired printer José Carlos Gianotti on hand to guide students in the use of one of their two Vandercook proofing presses.) Through the production of books and posters for local clinics and services, their ideas are transformed into solid and real pieces of communication, improving literacy skills and helping to prove to themselves and the community that they have something worthwhile to say.

Such work falls into a tradition, identified by Robin Kinross, of 'making it new with what is to hand', and in which can surely be found a positive message for design education in an era of climate emergency.[19] The pandemic is also perhaps a moment to re-evaluate the value of making, simply in relation to the well-being of our students. Pedagogically I have always felt that such arguments are too vulnerable to accusations of indulgence. Yet

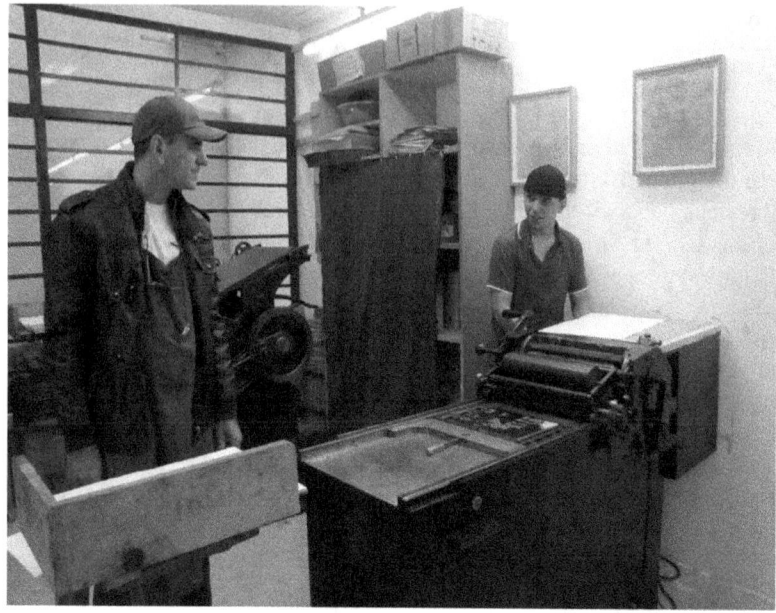

Figure P2.1 Retired Printer José Carlos Gianotti on Hand to Guide Students in Use of One of Their Two Vandercook Proofing Presses.

it was the stability of letterpress and the pleasure of making things by hand that led Juliet Shen's students to turn to it when faced with the uncertainty of the dot.com collapse.[20] The uncertainty generated by our current situation renders such findings more prescient than we could have previously imagined. After all, as Jan van Toorn has argued, a liberating pedagogy is one aligned with recovering forms of thinking and making useful, 'in the search for conditions that allow for a more truly human existence'.[21]

Notes

1 Robin Kinross, *Anthony Froshaug, documents of a life* (London: Hyphen, 2000), 70.
2 David Jury, *Reinventing print* (London: Bloomsbury, 2018), 172.
3 Eric Kindel, 'Letterpress: possibilities & practice', 16 March 2018, http://typography.network/2018/03/16/letterpress-possibilities-practice/.
4 Meredith Davis, '"Normal science" and the changing practices of design and design education', *Visible Language*, 50.1 (April 2016): 9; Bridgman (2002), in Stuart Bailey, *Towards a critical faculty* (New York: Parsons School of Design, Winter 2006/7).

5 Findeli, for example, rejects the 'fetishism of the artefact' in favour of a more human-centred context for design. In Bailey, *Towards a critical faculty*.
6 Raphael Cardoso, 'Craft versus design: moving beyond a tired dichotomy', in *The craft reader*, ed. Glenn Adamson (Oxford: Berg, 2010), 327.
7 A. Telier (Thomas Binder et al., eds.), *Design things* (Cambridge, MA: MIT, 2011), 11.
8 Daniel Charny, ed., *Power of making* (London: V&A, 2011), 40; Robin Fior, 'Recollections of designing and politics in London, 1957–1970', *Typography Papers*, no. 8 (2008), 140.
9 Charny, *Power of making*, 7.
10 Ibid, 51.
11 James Pallister, 'Press Association' in *Crafts*, no. 222 (Jan/February 2010), 38.
12 Quotation taken from the exhibition poster. (London: London College of Communication, 2009).
13 Robin Kinross, 'Letters in the city', *Eye*, no. 10 (1993), 69.
14 Wright's advances beyond the scope of existing teaching orthodoxies are noted in Ann Pillar, *Pop art and design*, ed. Anne Massey and Alex Seago (London: Bloomsbury, 2017), 137; Charny, *Power of making*, 51.
15 'Ane Thon Knutsen 22.01.19–27.01.19' last accessed 6 February 2021 https://kunstnerneshus.no/en/exhibitions/ane-thon-knutsen.
16 Neil Cummings, 'Socialised affection' in *Specialism*, ed. David Blamey (London: Occasional Table, 2016), 40–1.
17 Charny, *Power of making*, 49.
18 Ibid, 5.
19 Kinross, 'Letters in the city', 68.
20 Juliet Shen, *Resurrection of a reliance* (Seattle: School of Visual Concepts, 2007), 2.
21 Jan van Toorn, 'Deschooling and learning in design education', in *User-centred graphic design: mass communication and social change*, ed. J. Frascara (London: Taylor & Francis, 1997), 127.

4 The Role of the Letterpress Workshop

Rúben Dias and Sofia Meira

Nowadays we understand the historical importance of the technology of typography using movable type in the process of building the field of communication design. For a period spanning more than 500 years, it was one of the most effective means to compile, organise and disseminate information. Consequently, there is a vast amount of theoretical and technical information that is still relevant today.

We are interested in recovering and re-interpreting the universe of typography with movable type and its consequent application in higher education design contexts.

Existing information, which has a very demanding technical component and a high level of complexity, is now outdated. It is important to note that the former apprenticeship process primarily resulted from a workshop-school context in which the apprentice served under a master craftsman for several years until attaining autonomy. As a result of the computerisation of printing processes, this learning method was lost. The overwhelming majority of former typographers from the movable-type era left the *métier* several years ago. We are now left with the books and many technical manuals that are gradually being made available online, which have been out-of-print for many years. However, their preparation focused on a time when the typographer went through an extensive learning period, lasting several years and his life was to be a typographer, involving very different needs from those prevailing today.

The reconversion or implementation of the former printing houses into contemporary workshops and in particular into schools requires tremendous research work. New learning methods are required, adapted to a new reality. The current use of these typographic workshops now serves as a component to support a formal and plastic learning process that is no longer the main technique of graphic reproduction. After all, contemporary use has nothing to do with the use that existed in the golden age of movable type. Typography is no longer the principal means of graphic reproduction.

DOI: 10.4324/9781003173113-8

The path that led to the construction of that which we now define as a graphic communication designer was based on knowledge developed in the typographic workshops. The current concepts of composition used by the designers are an inescapable reflection of this, still present in today's technology through expressions such as Upper and Lower Case. The figure of the designer has replaced the typographer in the creative and technical side of the composition and its origins can be traced directly to typography.

> Tactility is a physical sensation and at the same time it is a mental experience; it is ambiguous in nature. In addition, the tactile object can both be hand-crafted from basic materials or produced using sophisticated technological and/or biochemical processes. In its growing complexity, tactility becomes ever more hybrid: layered in material, making the flowing sense of the tactile world increasingly ambiguous. What do we actually feel when we touch things?
>
> Freek Lomme, in *Effectuating Tactility and Print in the Contemporary*, page 5, 2015

The technology we use today highlights the origins of typography, and concepts such as *leading* are still used, which derives from the word *lead*. But leading also means the concept of direction, in the sense of a reading orientation. The leading is the space between lines that ensures continuity of reading from one line to the next. Digital typesetting tools observe a logic that structurally follows the concepts that were developed in the former workshops over several centuries.

The technology opens countless possibilities, while inevitably blocking certain features. In the past, the ability to sketch, create a project structure, lay foundations and make the full journey towards the final product was highly necessary and valued. Modern-day needs do not permit this, and computers perform these tasks.

Compositing with movable type implies a different way of thinking. Once the page size is defined on a computer, the blank page is taken for granted. This leads to the common misconception that one only has to add the graphic elements because the empty space is already there. This makes the empty spaces easily left as the overflowing and largely neglected element. When developing a typographic composition, physically with spaces and characters, it is necessary to place the furniture that represents the blank spaces which separate and organise the graphic elements – the text and image. The experience of this process enables the user to acquire an awareness of the "design" of the white space in the composition, simultaneously with the design of the text block.

The Role of the Letterpress Workshop   49

A comparison between past and present technology is pointless unless we can learn more from such a comparison. Manual printing offers a completely different experience from the digital environment. This exploration and material experimentation enables us to broaden the range of possibilities for the designer, from expanding the way of thinking or working methods, to the myriad of plasticity permitted by this technology. And this is just one example that contributes to the designer's training.

> Many of our biggest challenges appear to be heavily embedded in our current system of industrial production and consumption of designed and manufactured goods, and it is time for a reconsideration of what that same design tradition has put forward to alter and subvert this system.
>
> Marjanne van Helvert, in *The Responsible Object: A History of Design Ideology for the Future*, page 15, 2016

Currently, and largely supported by the Swiss school, the use of only one or two fonts or typographic families for each graphic project is promoted. This is a discreet register but at the same time a reductive and castrating formula for design, which has been widely imposed and contributed to the construction of a global trend. But typography has already revealed its potential by the typographic variety. It is worth noting how the Industrial Revolution led to an explosion in the production of fonts, as seen in the extensive font catalogues with an almost infinite typographic variety. In the late 19th century, the pantograph appeared throughout the western world. This made it possible to increase the production of fonts on a hitherto unseen scale. Companies such as Linotype, Monotype, or Portugal's Imprensa Nacional (to name just one local printing venture) emerged, producing types in unprecedented quantities and varieties. At this time, font catalogues were published with hundreds of pages, expanding the huge variety in body sizes and styles of fonts available in the market. Typographers, particularly since the late 19th century and early 20th century, developed complex compositions, which explored this rich variety. They used several totally different fonts in a single advertisement or entire pages with dozens of completely different typefaces. They composed pages with high graphic quality, based on the ability to communicate the message, as well as the formal balance adapted to the aesthetics of an era. This characteristic arose from the need to obtain visibility for each client with the resources that the workshops had at their disposal. Faced with all this variety, that was consolidated throughout the 20th century, only large workshops had the capacity to acquire complete sets of a typeface, in the various body sizes. Most workshops (small workshops) rarely had extensive typeface families. The possibility of downloading a font from the internet didn't yet exist. As a result, printers were obliged to sharpen their ingenuity and rediscover new solutions, using the typographic material they had at their disposal.

Notes for Implementing a Workshop in the 21st Century

The construction of a typography workshop in the current academic context can make a major contribution to the training of today's designers and is also relevant on several fronts, because it facilitates:

- Knowledge about the genesis of the designer's profession that is present in the means and techniques used today.
- Understanding of the evolution of technology and how it has influenced and may influence formal execution and contemporary graphic production.
- A formal experimentation through the physicality of fonts (as opposed to the digital environment).
- Plastic experimentation (besides the relationship with raw materials such as paper and ink) the implicit analogue process allows a much wider exploration of materials.
- Creating room for research on each of the above points.

It is also important to note that tactile learning involves two major components:

- Composition with physical objects. The relationship between moving characters, lines, vignettes, as well as the white material, which allows the printed elements to be organised and opens spaces for other forms of understanding and experimentation as opposed to the digital medium.
- Perception of the materiality of the print, associated with the technique (of the printer) making it possible to extend the experience of the designer who intends to work with the printed object. This is also associated with the characteristics of the variety of papers themselves, from their texture, opacity, bulk, as well as their workability when applied in different contexts.

Building a print workshop today requires evolution, in order to adjust it to a new audience. The current user goes through a brief learning process in a much more frivolous manner, compared to the situation that existed 50 years ago. We understand time in a very different way, which makes it necessary to adapt the working space and minimise the obstacles resulting from a lack of knowledge of the technique, in order to facilitate usage for those without any previous experience.

These new workspaces need new signage to facilitate the use of materials and instruments. Acquiring awareness of the various phases of the process improves the organisation of the project. A galley sheet makes it easier to compose and distribute the materials to their respective places. However, support from the technician will also be essential, in particular to help initiated users.

In the golden age of typography detailed identification of tools and materials was dispensable. It was through continuous experience that every printer got to know the workshop and its "secrets" like the back of his hand. These secrets served as tools that he would use throughout his life. It was about learning a *métier*. In today's digital age, when their use is much more fleeting and occasional, it is imperative to build mechanisms to facilitate the use of these materials. From the moment they are picked up to make the composition, until their redistribution after the end of the project.

Mapping the Type Case

Each language has its own type case which organises the characters in order to facilitate the composition. Marking the cases assists the less experienced user. This becomes particularly relevant since the contents of the boxes vary frequently. It is common for a case to have two fonts, one in the upper case and another in the lower case. In the old days this marking was unnecessary, mainly because of daily practice. Additionally, because of wear and tear on the type which would lead to its replacement, the use of the case also changed frequently.

Furniture Cabinets

The blank material is called leads and slugs, according to the respective thickness. Once again, usage by beginners can be difficult, given the large amount of sizes with very modest variety within the materials. Storage and identification in the cabinet, and the leads and slugs themselves, is another facilitating element for use and maintenance of the workshop.

The dimensions according to the Didot Point, in which the material is cast, make it possible to ascertain the length and thickness of each element, by using a type ruler. A mark placed on the width and height of the cabinet makes it possible to identify spaces intended for each length and thickness, and the correct placement to be physically and visually identified. However, its use can be facilitated.

The cabinet with shelves adjusted to the size of the material, makes it easier to maintain correct storage, highlighting when a shorter or longer element is placed on the wrong shelf. But this solution only resolves the question of length – the thickness of the material remains to be solved.

A mark applied to the leads and slugs makes it possible to improve their correct identification and highlight an incorrect placement.

The organisation and storage is also facilitated by a nick marking of the leads and slugs, or a numbering system for the furniture.

The way to ensure the longevity of these marks can be guaranteed through a relief marking on both tops, so that they are always visible when placed in the cabinet. These markings result from reinterpretation of the nick, or nicks already used in cast or wood type. They can now function as an identification, which makes it possible to facilitate the organisation of these materials. It is thereby possible to speed up the correct return to the cabinets, and the marking on the characters also facilitates correct placement in the composition.

Galley Sheet

The galley sheet is used to record the composition materials used throughout a job. It must also contain the user's identification and a contact. The information on the materials that are used makes it possible to identify where the respective elements were taken from – in particular the easel and its box.

This "document" helps the user easily locate the type case – either to reuse or distribute correctly and autonomously the characters, lines or ornaments in their respective boxes. If by chance he does not return to the workshop to distribute the material, this information enables anyone to restitute the elements used.

In a workshop context, the composition process supports the creative process, in the exploration of typographic options, both in type, lines, ornaments and in blank material. The systematisation on galley sheets contributes to a methodological construction of the user. The systematic recording enables analysis as well as understanding of the materials used, increasing awareness of the creative process.

Type Cabinets

The fonts are stored in type cases which are organised in type cabinets. Their identification becomes relevant to keep the workshop organised. It is even more important to ensure that this organisation is genuinely useful to the user. It is important to remember that a school workshop today is essentially intended for inexperienced users.

Alphabetical identification of each cabinet and numbering for each type case makes it possible to identify their correct placement. The practical use of such a solution would end up revealing that a type case was easily changed from one cabinet to another.

The addition of a graphic system for marking type cases, with an exclusive graphic design per cabinet, ensures that each type case belongs to only one set.

However, the attribution of a letter to each cabinet and a number to each box is still relevant, and makes it possible to improve the organisation of the workshop and speed up its cataloguing and identification on the galley sheet.

This is still a growing and building process, which evolves according to the needs of the workshop's day-to-day life. The new uses of a workshop imply differences in the organisation and use of the workspace. These adaptations enhance new uses, in this new context, but it is important to give continuity to that which already exists.

Typography workshops often had a generous collection of catalogues. From type catalogues, paper, to finishing materials for special prints such as hot foils or binding fabrics. They were usually – and still are today – offered by suppliers to workshops, design agencies and studios. The implementation of a graphic library provided access to these materials and even the way that they are used, still in this environment. Finally, it also permits the exploration potential of a multitude of material aspects to be expanded.

The addition of books to explore these techniques also enables close discussion with technicians, in accordance with the workshop and machinery available.

Final Considerations

One contribution that should be highlighted is the ability of the workshop space to produce study and work tools, in order to recover these technologies as a laboratory for experimentation and exploration and open a space towards building knowledge through applied research on the technique – from design to history.

Naturally, most of these projects take a long time to be implemented. However, in some cases they may prove to be economical, enabling processes to provide direct contact between conceptualisation, implementation and the final product. The designer's personalised intervention in the production process contributes to the perspective of the "Designer Craftsman". Access to this technology enables a better compression and cause-effect relationship between conception and actual execution, amplifying the user's knowledge in real time. It makes it possible to avoid the time lag between the digital conception and the reception of the project produced in the factory.

Some designers are particularly interesting for the way they direct their skills and energies and for the way they contextualise their own practice. Others are fascinating by the way they find creative solutions and the critical thinking that this involves.

Andrew Howard, conversation with José Bártolo – Pli* Arte & Design magazine n°1 Summer 2011, pp. 34–38.

Setting up a workshop is only the beginning of a process. To improve the organisation by enhancing its use and maintenance adapted to the present-day context is a necessity that will enhance its use. Trying to make the composition process more agile will undoubtedly make it easier to use for an inexperienced user, and will be sufficient to foster interest in its use. The real challenge is to build teaching methods adapted to a "digital generation". Taking into account that, even if the members of this generation have something to gain from this way of learning, they tend to take refuge in the agility of digital processes.

The aim is not to deny the use or advantages of current technologies such as the computer, or the evolution of digital media. Instead, it seeks to emphasise that they are tools and that there is an entire range of other options available. By crossing the various philosophies, from analogue practice to the digital revolution, the aim is to promote and expand their possibilities.

In this learning workshop environment, it is possible to reconcile the use of the various processes – analogue and digital, far from the pressure of a business oriented to the optimisation of resources. Here it is possible to explore graphic and productive possibilities, which make it possible to bring something new to the present day.

New processes for the implementation of movable type are widespread, as are other tools and the contiguous use of current printing methods. New training methods and involvement with the academic context are also emerging.

Valuing the tools and the technique of typography with movable type, we believe in learning in a workshop-based and experience-driven approach to design, of course allied to digital tools and analogue and digital innovation. It is interesting to recognise the importance of letterpress studies for the interpretation and understanding of current design teaching issues.

Bibliography

da Silva Libânio, 1908. *Manual do Tipógrafo*, Biblioteca de Instrução Profissional, Lisbon.

Dias, Ruben and Meira, Sofia, 2018. *Imprimere, Arte e Processo Anos 250 anos da Imprensa Nacional*, Imprensa Nacional and Esad–Idea, Portugal.

Dias, Rúben and Monteiro, Joana, 2016. *Manual Prático do Tipógrafo*, Editora dos Tipos, Coimbra, Portugal.

Heller, Steven and Talarico, Lita, 2008. *The Design Entrepreneur: Turning Graphic Design Into Goods That Sell*, Rockport Publishers, Inc., United States of America.

Lomme, Freek, 2016. *Effectuating Tactility and Print in the Contemporary*, Onomatopee 118, Eindhoven.

Ludovico, Alessandro, 2012. *Post-digital Print – The Mutation of Publishing since 1894*, Onomatopee 77, Rotterdam.

Maravelas, Paul, 2010. *Letterpress Printing, a Manual for Modern Fine Printers*, Oak Knoll, New Castle, Delaware.

Marchetti, A., 1951. *O Impressor Tipográfico*, vol. 1. Lisboa: Biblioteca Profissional Salesiana Oficinas de São José.

———, 1956. *O Impressor Tipográfico*, vol. 2. Lisboa: Biblioteca Profissional Salesiana, Oficinas de São José.

———, 1960. *O Impressor Tipográfico*, vol. 5. Lisboa: Biblioteca Profissional Salesiana, Oficinas de São José.

———, 1971. *O Impressor Tipográfico*, vol. 3. Lisboa: Biblioteca Profissional Salesiana, Oficinas de São José.

———, 1973. *O Impressor Tipográfico*, vol. 4. Lisboa: Biblioteca Profissional Salesiana, Oficinas de São José.

Queiroz, Maria Inês, José, Inês and Ferreira, Diogo, 2019. *Indústria, Arte e Letras. 250 Anos da Imprensa Nacional*, Imprensa Nacional, Lisbon.

Ryder, John, 1976. *Printing for Pleasure*, The Bodley Head, London.

van Helvert, Marjanne, 2016. *The Responsible Object – A History of Design Ideology for the Future*, Marjanne van Helvert, Amsterdam.

5 From Letterpress to Screen
Learning from a Modular Type System

*Roberto Gamonal Arroyo and
Andreu Balius Planelles*

Introduction

When we think about modularity, we often consider simple structures defined as single elements that exist to become part of a more complex structure. Modules join each other in a logical manner, following a set of given rules.

We can understand type composition as a way to combine modules, where each piece of metal works as a module in the composing of a paragraph of text. Designing simple pieces and combining them together, creating the shape of a letter, is a quick way to 'draw' letters (if we understand drawing from a very open perspective).

Teaching the basics of type design using the concept of modularity is a good way to introduce students to the process of creating letter shapes. Not all students are sufficiently good at drawing letters through lettering. Defining relations among letters in terms of spacing, contrast, modulation and proportions also requires a trained eye.

Modules, as single basic pieces (based on geometry or otherwise), are much easier to draw and work with. By combining, we follow basic rules. The coherence of the result has to do with the design of the modular system. The visual relationship between the single modular elements contributes to the general harmony and unity of the result.

Working with modules helps us understand how parts of letters are related to each other and how designing an alphabet is a process of combining shapes consistently. Concepts such as proportions, contrast, modularity, counterforms, spacing and the basics of type anatomy can easily be acquired while building letter shapes.

Modularity is a logical and constructive way of thinking and action that is integrated into a design system. Perhaps one of the most perfect design systems is moveable type. It is no accident that it has survived almost unchanged for five centuries.

Super Tipo Veloz

Super Tipo Veloz (or simply, Super Veloz) was a modern-conceived type system created by the Catalan printer and typographer, Joan Trochut (1920–1980), in the late 1930s as a tool to improve visual graphics in small commercial printed matter such as letterheads, logo design, dropcaps, custom lettering and other typographical works (Balius, 2007). It was produced and distributed by José Iranzo Foundry (Barcelona) in 1942 (Figure 5.1).

Super Veloz was based on a concept of modularity where the idea of type composition was shifted to the idea of type design. Each typeface was a glyph, a single component of a letter rather than a complete letter in itself, which could be combined with other glyphs to produce custom-built letterforms, even illustrations and ornaments.

It was a great help for local printers in Spain's post-Civil war period. Despite the shortage of material, they could be self-sufficient to perform original and creative works using a single typeface. The most common jobs that small printers used to do with this typeface was the creation of

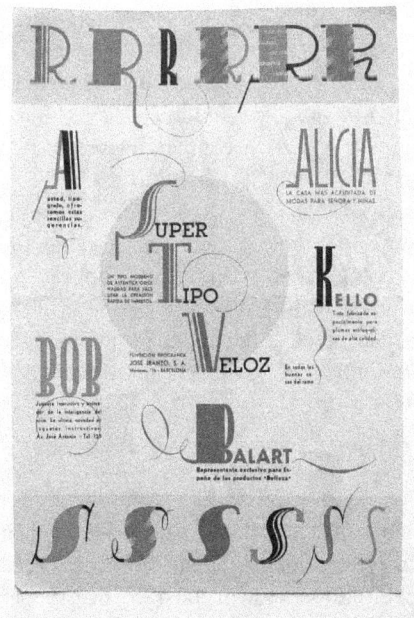

Figure 5.1 Promotional Sheet of Super Tipo Veloz Showing its Many Combination Possibilities (Between 1942 and 1945 Approximately).

letterheads for business cards, because they could create logos themselves without the need for a draughtsman (Martínez Sicluna, 1945: 208).

Nevertheless, Super Veloz was not that simple. It was a complex modular system with more than 300 modules classified and grouped in three collections, three supplementary sets and calligraphic features. The most basic ones could be reduced to a smaller number of shapes. The rest of them were conceived as terminals, ornaments and swashes, and single flourishing calligraphic elements to be used for decorative purposes.

Looking at the printed results, it doesn't seem to be built by modules because it fails to respond to the strict geometry of other typefaces that several foundries marketed years before, such as *Futura Schmuck* by Bauersche Giesserei, *Elementare Schmuckformen* by Stempel AG, *Vignettes Décors* by the Fonderie Typographique Française, *Fregio Gloria* by Fausto Galico Fonderia and *Geometric Figures* by Fundición José Iranzo (Gamonal, 2017). Although Super Veloz follows a modular logic, its appearance is neither mechanical nor rigid. Taking into account previous modular experiences, it is one of the most sophisticated. Designs created using Super Veloz have decorative and calligraphic reminiscences that remind us of Art Deco printed samples.

Super Veloz is much more than a typeface. It incorporates many typefaces in one and serves for something more than creating letters. Some examples of use on different graphic solutions may be seen in the NOVADAM volumes,[1] edited by Joan Trochut and his father, Ettienne. In its pages a great variety of typesetting compositions demonstrated the huge possibilities and combinations permitted by Super Veloz. These NOVADAM volumes also explained how modules had been combined and which ones were used to achieve it.

A digital version of Super Veloz was designed in 2004 by Andreu Balius and Àlex Trochut (Joan's grandson) for desktop publishing, using the facilities that font editors such as Fontographer and FontLab applications provided by the 1990s. The digital version faithfully follows the original designs, and the fonts are currently distributed at the Typerepublic foundry (www.typerepublic.com) in different collections under the same name and number as they were released in 1942.

Work Approaches

One of the main goals of this experience is to introduce Spanish Modernism and Joan Trochut's idea of modularity to students, together with his type design work. Beyond its historical relevance, we consider that Super Veloz's great versatility, dual figurative and textual capacity and its systematic nature means that its use is likely to become a method for learning in typographic design.

Our work objective considers this modular system as a useful and understandable method for a comprehensive introduction to type design. This may be plausible because its modular nature enables the performance of various operations that multiply its combinatorial possibilities through addition, deletion, repetition, rotation, overlap, substitution, inversion, etc. Its constructive character also allows us to understand the different components with which the letter is constructed, since its modules can be related to parts of the typographic anatomy.

As a tool based on modular shapes we find them to be an engaging playground instrument for students in the practice of type design. Building letterforms from some of the basic modules of Super Veloz and other components from its type collection makes it easy to understand the basics of type design and the alphabet as a system.

In spite of the complexity of more than 300 modules, we can reduce it to a basic set of 70. The rest provide a second level of possibilities to the working process.

When working with a basic element set, such as squares, circles and triangles, it provides excessively basic results. By contrast, Super Veloz provides greater complexity and thereby facilitates less formal structures. It also enables greater experimentation as an approach to type design based on modules.

Working with Students

On the basis of our practice and knowledge of this innovative modular type system in different media, from digital to analogue training, we have conveyed this experience to students and the general public through workshops and design classes.

The constructive and playful spirit of Super Veloz means that it can also be used not only among design students, but also members of the general public, including both adults and children.

We will highlight several cases where the didactic and creative potential of Super Veloz has been put into practice.

The first documented evidence we have of the use of Super Veloz in an educational context was in the Graphic Design degree at the Buenos Aires University, in Rubén Fontana's Typography classes (Cátedra Fontana, 1996: 58–59)

In order to test our goals we developed different methodologies, depending on the medium used.

In the first stage, Super Veloz is introduced to students in order to familiarise them with the modular system and how it used to work. This is a good approach, not only to introduce the context of Modern type design in Spain but also to show the possibilities of letterpress printing as an experimental medium for design practices.

In the second stage, students are provided with the modules that they are then supposed to work with to build up letters. In this stage, an introductory class on type design basics is taught to help students during the work process.

Finally, the results are exhibited to be analysed and commented on by both teachers and students, in order to draw conclusions and consolidate knowledge.

Letterpress Workshop

Students learned the basic concepts of type composition for letterpress printing using the Super Veloz modules. The most challenging part in the typesetting process was the adjustments of blank metal pieces since the modules have different sizes and, when placing them, the usual horizontality of the text is not followed. Beyond Super Veloz's ability to build images, the importance of white space was appreciated as an active element since it could be touched and felt as a physical component of the composition. One of our most important conclusions is that Super Veloz ['*Super Fast' type*] is not as fast as its 'name' suggests: it is actually very time-consuming.

Super Veloz Online

Nowadays, there are very few collections of Super Veloz still available in letterpress workshops. Most of these fonts were the first to be thrown away when offset printing took over traditional letterpress practices. Lead metal types were sold as scrap metal for some easy money when the printing houses had to shut down.

SuperVeloz.net[2] is an online application that everyone can work with, using digital outlines. It is based on the digitised version of Super Veloz designed in 2004, which allows students (and other users) to combine all modules on screen, then create a single design and save it into a public online Gallery. The idea to translate physical modules to digital outlines came after thinking about a more contemporary use of this modular system and provided a way to put into the hands of any user the possibility to get to know and use it, while having fun.

It has been used by a fairly large number of schools in Spain as a class exercise as far as we can ascertain from teachers' feedback.

In this online platform, it is not possible to distort or modify the modules. Only scaling and turning is possible in order to maintain the original physical shapes, while providing the possibilities of digital drawing software.

Digital to Letterpress

This workshop combined the possibilities of digital graphic design with the limits of analogue physical letterpress technology. The objective for this workshop was the creation of a Bestiary formed by illustrations of animals made with the modules of Super Veloz. Students started their sketching process with a digital version of Super Veloz using digital tools such as Adobe Illustrator and afterwards they had to translate their sketches (whatever they were) into the composition room. Students experienced the different language and limitations in each tool. For example they learned that letterpress has its own rules in terms of modular standardisation, but on the other hand it has the expressiveness of printed ink on paper. Also adapting computer-based designs into letterpress typesetting can be very tricky and requires some compromises.

For the workshop, free test licenses of digital Super Veloz were provided to all participants.

Laser Cut Super Veloz

In order to be able to give a workshop on Super Veloz at the London College of Communication (University of the Arts, London) in June 2017, for logistical and technical reasons, a laser cutting of a selection of pieces had to be done. From the more than 300 modules, a total of 64 modules were selected, with different sizes, shapes and thicknesses that were cut to twice their original size, to create large letters.

Seven students of the BA Hons degree course in Graphic and Media Design were chosen for their interest in typography and having previously taken the foundational course in letterpress. During three days in four-hour sessions we worked in the printing office of the educational centre, with the goal of designing, composing and printing a commemorative poster for the 75th anniversary of Super Veloz, illustrated with an alphabet created with decorative and ornamental letters made using its modules.

Again, the crossing of analogue and digital technologies was very interesting. The integration of the different letters made by the students was also enriching since it demonstrated the enormous combinatorial capacity despite having reduced the number of modules to a quarter.

Stencilled Devices

Other experiences have turned this modular type system into stencilled devices. Stencils are easy tools to work with and provide sufficient room for freedom and inventiveness.

Following the selection of modules from the previous workshop, the idea of creating a stencil emerged. The ordering of these modules revealed that the positive forms hid negative forms that could be cut to create a simple and accessible tool to draw and sketch without the need for knowledge of calligraphy or typography. This ease of use has made it possible to test the Super Veloz stencil with excellent results amongst adults and children. Despite the complexity of a typographic system such as Super Veloz, children can perfectly assimilate its dual textual capacity, creating their name and their figurative capacity when creating illustrations.

Since it is about outlining the parts of a letter to put them in relation to others, it also makes it possible to explore the technique of lettering.

Super Veloz, despite being a modular typeface, has a very pronounced calligraphic flavour. Therefore, the plastic and ornamental features of the letters can also be explored.

The objective of this stencilled workshop was to develop the design of a word or concept based on the technique of lettering using the Super Veloz modules. Workshop attendees start with their modules and then freely complete the design with ligatures, flourishes, shadows, volume, etc. made by themselves manually.

Rubber Stamps

Another way that the Super Veloz modules were applied was to use them as rubber stamps, inking and printing them on a surface. With this playful solution, the main goal was to produce cupholders.

This workshop combined both designing and printing in a very naive manner. Each module was reproduced and cut as a rubber stamp. It was mounted on a transparent methacrylate base that made it possible to see where the stamp was positioned and facilitated the overlapping of modules to create more playful compositions. This is a very easy-going way to experiment with this system.

Motion Graphics

A more contemporary use of Super Veloz in motion graphics workshops has turned this dynamic system into a kinetic typographical experience. Using Adobe After Effects and other dynamic software for motion graphics, letters were built up in movement.

The methodologies were basically the same, even though the medium and software were different.

Students were provided with the digital font files and they had to sketch and figure out how to build letters using the modular set. They defined a colour palette to unify how colour was used throughout the entire film. They had to pick up a piece of music to help with the rhythm and movement of the letter compositions and create a kinetic alphabet film, from A to Z. Each letter was assembled in movement with different modules and faded out into a new one. Time and rhythm were important elements when building letters in motion.

This work was conceived as a collaborative project among students, where they had to set timings, define a narrative structure and distribute the letters.

Conclusion

Super Veloz has had many lives over its almost 80-year history. It has gone from lead to vectors, from printing to screen. It has been cast, vectorised and laser cut. It has moved from analogue to digital and vice versa. All these techniques and methodologies have been used in the workshops, supporting and mixing each other.

The limitations imposed by analogue techniques helped people become aware of the creative and constructive process of the typographic form and the blank space that not only surrounds it but also sustains it. Digital techniques enable greater freedom and presuppose a break that transcends physical materiality results. The combination of the two makes them complement and multiply their possibilities.

Nevertheless, both technical and historical information on Super Veloz is presented to all participants. The only thing that changes is the medium used – original metal type or digitised modules as vectors for creating letters on screen, dynamic or static – and the support – paper or screen.

In all these different ways of working with Super Veloz, three ways of building letters come together: typography, calligraphy and lettering. It engages students and provides a more experimental approach at first sight.

Through the use of Super Veloz, students can approach the basics of both type design and lettering. The results are not intended for reading text sizes, but for a more ornamental and experimental communicational approach.

From our research and practical workshop experiences, we can conclude that Super Veloz is a useful tool for educational purposes that links traditional movable type concepts to digital type design with creativity driving results. It is a typographic system ahead of its time and has been able to adapt to changes and new formats. Its prodigious versatility has made it a model of learning based on modularity for students in the 21st century.

Notes

1 NOVADAM states for 'New Documentary Archive of Modern Art'.

2 The application was built to run on Adobe Flash player, which used to be an essential complement to surf the Internet at that time. Unfortunately, Flash player has become obsolete on web browsers since December 31, 2020, and the possibilities to use Super Veloz online through this platform is now limited to old browser versions.

References

Balius, A. (2007). *SuperVeloz: A creative response to an emergency situation*. Ultrabold (2) London: St. Bride Library, pp 6–9.

Balius, A. and Trochut. A. (2004). *Super-Veloz: Un tipo moderno*. Madrid: Blur Ediciones.

Balius, A. (2003). SuperVeloz: Modernism, in the Spanish way. http://superveloz.net/historia_en.php.

Catopodis, M. (2014). *Tipometría. Las medidas en diseño gráfico*. Valencia: Campgràfic.

Cuesta, M. y Duró, J. (2009). The art of necessity. *Creative Review 4*, 40–43.

Del Hoyo Arjona, J. (2001). *El módulo tipográfico. Aproximaciones a su conocimiento contemplado desde la compresión, el estudio, el análisis y la catalogación sistemática de la obra de Juan Trochut Blanchard* (tesis doctoral). Spain: Universidad de Barcelona.

Fontana, C. (1996). *Pensamiento tipográfico*. Buenos Aires: Edicial.

Gamonal Arroyo, R. (2017). Super Tipo Veloz: la tipografía supercalifragilística. https://pionerosgraficos.com/la-tipografia-supercalifragilistica/.

Martínez Sicluna, V. (1945). *Teoría y práctica de la Tipografía*. Barcelona: Gustavo Gili

Trochut, E. y Trochut, J. (1954). *Abundancia. Catálogo de las colecciones de piezas Super-Veloz*. Barcelona: Fundición Tipográfica José Iranzo.

Typerepublic (2019). SuperVeloz. http://www.typerepublic.com/fonts/superveloz.

6 PDLPX: The Post-Digital Letterpress Print Exchange
Methodological Innovation in the Exploration of Contemporary Letterpress Practice

Chris Wilson

Over recent years letterpress has increasingly been employed by artists and designers as a conspicuous alternative to established digital technologies (Jury, 2004; Suzuki, 2011; Williamson, 2013). The medium is being employed by design educators as a catalyst to instil creativity and convey design conventions to their students (Cooper, Gridneff and Haslam, 2014; Rigley, 2005). Other practitioners, such as Anthony Burrill (Tate, 2016) and Amos Paul Kennedy Jr (Fulleylove, 2020), are printing with archaic analogue techniques to signal a reassessment of modern technology and the culture that it represents. This study focuses on an alternative and more progressive approach taken by a growing number of creative practitioners who are integrating analogue and digital technology through the appropriation of letterpress within their practice (Fleishman, 2017; Double Dagger, 2020). These explorative endeavours reappraise the traditional techniques of letterpress by combining relief printing with a range of digital manufacturing techniques, including 3D printing, CNC machining and lasercutting. Notable examples of such practice include A23D from New North Press (New North Press, 2020), Thomas Mayo's laser-engraved woodtype (Hamilton Wood Type Museum, 2020), experimental type production at p98a typographic workshop (p98a, 2016) and Dafi Kühne's creative poster work (Kühne, 2017).

Letterpress printing has become synonymous with handicraft and traditional methods of reproduction (Jury, 2006). Along with many of its associated crafts, letterpress has been superseded by digital technologies as a means of mass production. However, analogue printing persists, despite digital technologies becoming a ubiquitous and intrinsic aspect of contemporary life (Jandrić, 2019; Striano, 2019). Predictions of the death of analogue print reproduction have proven not only to have been premature

DOI: 10.4324/9781003173113-10

but failed to acknowledge the inherent value of analogue technology (Chen Design Associates, 2006; Luckman, 2015; Massumi, 2002; Sundén, 2015).

Following the digital revolution being classified as historical (Negroponte, 1998), the term 'post-digital' has emerged to 'acknowledge the current state of technology' (Pepperell and Punt, 2000, p.2). The Post-digital Letterpress Print Exchange (PDLPX) was undertaken to investigate why contemporary letterpress practitioners are integrating digital technology into their practice. The established format of a print exchange was combined with a survey methodology to create a research method capable of gathering relevant insight into practice and practitioners. The study contributes to ongoing research into how contemporary letterpress practice is influenced by the post-digital age (Wilson, 2021).

Print Exchange Format

Exchanging printed artwork is a common activity among communities of printers. Artwork is regularly shared among practitioners as a social and collaborative interaction. Print exchanges provide a structured process for sharing original artwork, often employing a thematic or curated approach. Letterpress printers have a long history of circulating their work as a means of disseminating practice knowledge and broadcasting individual skill, style or creative processes. A notable historical example is *The Printers' International Specimen Exchange* (Young, 2012), which was launched in London in 1880 and became an influential institution that fostered the advancement of technical and artistic skill within the print industry. Many small-scale exchanges operate today, each maintaining or enabling communities of practitioners while facilitating the dissemination of knowledge and skill among their members (Fine Press Book Association, 2020; Hot Bed Press, 2020; International Print Exchange, 2020).

A typical print exchange will be aligned thematically, either by subject or technique, and require participating printmakers to create an edition of original prints for submission. Once all of the participants have submitted an edition, they are distributed into sets that contain a print from each edition. These sets or 'exchange portfolios' are then sent to each participant, enabling them to review the collective responses of all those taking part in the exchange. Although it is a common activity within printmaking, the use of a print exchange to gather data within a research context has not been widely documented. Print communities represent a rich source of experience and knowledge of practice. Harnessing the conventions of an exchange format as a means of surveying practice presents an opportunity to conduct research through a direct collaboration with practitioners. The latter's familiarity with the format and requirements of engaging with an exchange make it an appropriate and accessible format for studying their practice.

Print Exchange Research Method

A traditional exchange portfolio contextualises individual work within a broader community of practice. When applied to an academic study as a research method the format enables further direct comparison and analysis to explore an identified phenomenon. A combination of text-based and printed responses from practitioners provides a study with units of analysis (Patton, 2002, p.228). Gathering printed artwork in addition to a questionnaire survey generates a rich corpus of data which can be analysed to build theory using insights drawn from examples of practice, tacit knowledge, studio activity and participant experience.

To operate an exchange requires access to, and ideally membership of, a practice community. The more a researcher is familiar with the practice being studied and its active community, the better an exchange's design can be tailored to effectively engage practitioners. An established familiarity with the creative processes, technologies and techniques integral to a practice provides the researcher with the requisite awareness of how to suitably conduct their enquiry. Additionally, relevant individual understanding and tacit knowledge of practice will enhance the researcher's 'theoretical sensitivity' (Strauss and Corbin, 1990, p.41), supporting their integration within a participating community.

Integrating within a community of practice will inevitably result in a researcher becoming somewhat invested with the group's values and biases. This influence on a researcher is an inevitable challenge to 'value-neutrality' (Bhaskar, 1989, p.62). Attention should be given to the researcher's reflexivity throughout the research study and particularly during the analysis stage through a process of continual self-awareness (May and Perry, 2014, p.109). The multiple sources of data collected by the exchange can also be used to authenticate a study through triangulation of empirical results (Eisenhardt, 1989, p.532). A balance must be sought between sensitivity, acquired through a researcher's immersion within a practice community, and the potential biases that their integration as a practitioner-researcher might impose upon the data collected or development of theory (Le Gallais, 2008, p.145–155; Koch, 2006, p.91–103).

Gaining access to a community and familiarity with production practices and obtaining applicable practical skills present substantial obstacles to a researcher uninitiated in the specific area of interest. A researcher will require significant time and concerted effort to immerse themselves in a research subject to the level described. Although this immersion will provide many benefits, the demands of this investment may understandably discourage the use of exchange if a researcher's resources are constrained.

Applying the Exchange Method

The 'Letterpress Workers' network was identified as an appropriate community for study since their members exemplify a range of approaches to contemporary letterpress. A representative sample of artists, designers and printers who employ both digital and analogue technology in their letterpress practice was invited to participate in the exchange (Patton, 2002, p.236). The exchange method was applied to survey participating practitioners by requesting that they respond to its common theme by producing original printed artwork. In addition to the exchange's title theme, a series of open questions were posed to prompt participants' printed responses (what is post-digital letterpress, how has letterpress changed and adapted, why do we continue to print using this technique?). Participants also completed questionnaires that collected a written record of their individual creative process, print production and perception of analogue and digital technology being used within their practice.

The PDLPX was launched in June 2017 at the Letterpress Workers International Summit (Letterpress Workers, 2017) in Milan, Italy. This annual event brings letterpress practitioners from across the world together to print small editions, present projects and foster further collaboration within a growing community of letterpress printers. During a presentation at the event, the researcher introduced the study and announced an open call to participate in the exchange. A total of 30 printers declared an interest in taking part and were provided with an exchange documentation pack. This contained an invitation to participate, explaining the exchange theme and an overview of the project. A participant information sheet, questionnaire and consent letter were also included. These documents were contained in an unassembled 24 cm square box, pre-labelled with a return postage address. Participants were required to respond to the invitation by producing an original letterpress printed edition of 30 prints and deliver them using the postage box. The exchange was launched with a six-month deadline. A reminder email was sent to all practitioners three months prior to the deadline. This was intended to highlight the remaining time before submissions were due and gather definitive confirmations from participation. Fifteen practitioners responded to this email to confirm their participation, of which 12 submitted to the exchange.

As intended, the resulting exchange portfolios compiled artwork printed using an array of traditional and post-digital letterpress techniques. The rationale directing each creative response and details of its production was captured in the accompanying questionnaire. Artwork submitted to the exchange was printed using matrices created using photopolymer, laser-cutting, laser engraving, CNC milling and 3D printing techniques. Traditional movable type and woodtype were also used, along with a number of instances of found objects that were improvised to print modular elements within a design (Figure 6.1).

The exchange portfolios document aspects of the collective creativity, skill and personal motivations shared by a community of practice. Responses submitted to the study were analysed using constructivist grounded theory (Charmaz, 2006). The researcher compiled written descriptions of each printed submission, which document both the physical attributes and appearance of each artwork, along with the conceptual meaning it communicates. The researcher used their practice knowledge and sensitivity to interpret these qualities, supported by the participants' written descriptions. Constructivist grounded theory was applied to enabled theory to emerge from the data (Charmaz, 2008; Strauss and Corbin, 1990; Glaser, 1978). Each submission was initially analysed at the level of individual sentences and sentence groups, using open coding to identify units

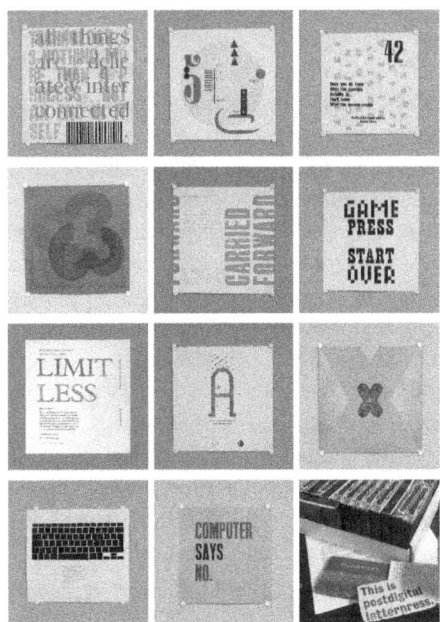

Figure 6.1 The 12 Prints Submitted to the Exchange.

of meaning (Goulding, 1998, p.53). These open codes were condensed and refined using secondary coding, coalescing them into a smaller number of abstract concepts. Through selective coding, concepts were organised into four theoretical categories: (a) Building a Forme, (b) Printing is Boring, (c) Playing within the Rules, and (d) Digilog Prints. Attributes were identified for each of these categories, enabling constant comparative analysis of participant submissions (Merriam and Associates, 2002; Mills, Bonner and Francis 2006).

Results

The submitted artwork and questionnaire responses revealed dynamic relational factors driving post-digital letterpress practice. The results demonstrate that letterpress practitioners are engaging with analogue print technology as a means of directing their creative practice and focusing their making process. Digital technology is integrated into this process by following established conventions, augmenting existing methods of printing by supplementing rather than subverting letterpress practice. Participants reported different career experiences, applications of letterpress techniques, and perceptions of digital and analogue technology yet possessed corresponding values and engaged in similar forms of practice, providing credibility to the emergent theory. The categories that form the study's results are now summarised with illustrative quotations from the participants.

Building a Forme describes practitioners' application of technology to construct a design by hand. The term 'forme' refers to an assembled composition of metal type. Practitioners value the essential physicality that letterpress provides. Elizabeth and John commented, 'Typesetting, imposition and printing all by hand gives us a level of control and creativity that we can only find through letterpress'. Letterpress presents a literal physical analogue of typography through systems of movable type. This property is exemplified by Thomas, 'For me typography is two-dimensional architecture. When I build my formes, I build a flat house'. Practitioners contrasted analogue print technology with digital or virtual alternatives as providing greater immediacy and direct control through tangible resistance.

Printing is Boring acknowledges the emphasis practitioners place on the creative design process facilitated by letterpress techniques. John explained, 'I cannot be described as a jobbing printer, primarily the practice is about creativity'. The labour of print production is recognised as intrinsic to letterpress, but the artistic challenge and creativity essential in physically composing a printed artwork provide the principal appeal. A position expounded by Marie: 'I love letterpress. I love using it. But I don't want to be a printer'. Contemporary letterpress printers are primarily designers of original prints above being producers of printed material. Practitioners engage letterpress technology and the design process it facilitates to focus and direct their creative design process. Carl put it simply, 'Well it's not about production here. It is about design'.

Playing within the Rules categorises a tension identified between the creative vision of a practitioner and the restrictions imposed by the conventions of letterpress technology. These constraints are embraced as a catalyst for creativity and innovation. John reported that 'I find the constraints presented by letterpress in terms of working solely with the objects available to me actually enables a greater creativity than the digital process'. The creative challenge provided by engaging with the intrinsic limitations of established systems of production initiates a dialogue between the maker and their equipment. This interaction influences the aesthetic form and composition of the printed outcome, Giacomo described the procedure, 'I think using my hands, fighting the physical limitations of an analogue process, can be a real way to enhance my work'. Practitioners demonstrate their skill by successfully navigating these restrictions to realise a design that communicates their intended message as a 'well printed' artwork. Richard illustrated this experience, 'It feels like being stranded on an island and making your own shelter'.

Conclusion

PDLPX was successful in collecting a diverse range of printed responses on the theme of post-digital letterpress (Figure 6.1). The exchange enabled exploration of the post-digital age's influence on contemporary letterpress practice and the results of the study have contributed towards the development of a grounded theory of post-digital letterpress practice (Wilson, 2021). Application of the exchange method demonstrated its potential to collect rich data by engaging with practitioners. Submissions to the exchange provided examples of post-digital practice, supplemented with accounts of their creation and the practitioners' motivations. Analysis resulted in the generation of theoretical categories that describe the phenomenon of post-digital letterpress practice. The exchange method provides a highly adaptable means of studying arts, design or craft practice with networks and communities.

The author gratefully acknowledges the generous support and cooperation of the letterpress practitioners who made the PDLPX possible.

Richard Ardagh, New North Press, *United Kingdom*
Matthias Beck, Tipos en su tinta, *Tenerife, Spain*
John Christopher, Flowers & Fleurons, *United Kingdom*

Elizabeth Ellis & David Marshall, The Counter Press, *United Kingdom*
Armina Ghazaryan, Type & Press, *Belgium*
Thomas Gravemaker, LetterpressAmsterdam, *The Netherlands*
Hannah Harkes, Labora, *Estonia*
Claudio Madella, Goodtypes, *Italy*
Carl Middleton, Neat Design, *United Kingdom*
Giacomo Silva, *Italy*
Marie Vandevoorde, *Belgium*

References

Bhaskar, R. (1989). *The possibility of naturalism.* (2nd ed.). Hemel Hampstead: Harvest.

Charmaz, C. (2006) *Constructing grounded theory: A practical guide through qualitative analysis.* London: Sage.

Charmaz, K. (2008) Constructionism and the grounded theory method. In J. A. Holstein, and J. F. Gubrium (Eds.), *Handbook of constructionist research* (pp. 397–412). New York: The Guilford Press.

Chen Design Associates (2006) *Fingerprint: The art of using hand-made elements in graphic design.* New York: HOW.

Cooper, A., Gridneff, R. and Haslam, A. (2014) Letterpress: Looking backward to look forward. *Visible Language* 47(3): 52–72.

Double Dagger (2020) About — Double Dagger — Letterpress printing in the digital age. Retrieved 24 November 2020, from https://www.doubledagger.co/about/

Eisenhardt, K. M. (1989) Building theories from case study research. *Academy of Management Review* 14(4): 532–550.

Fine Press Book Association (2020) Parenthesis. Retrieved 15 November 2020, from http://b7s.677.myftpupload.com/parenthesis/.

Fleishman, G. (2017) How letterpress printing came back from the dead | Backchannel, *Wired*. Retrieved 23 December 2020, from https://www.wired.com/story/how-letterpress-printing-came-back-from-the-dead/

Fulleylove, R. (2020) How I got here: Amos Paul Kennedy Jr, *Creative Review*. Retrieved 24 August 2020, from https://www.creativereview.co.uk/how-i-got-here-amos-paul-kennedy-jr/.

Glaser, B. (1978) *Theoretical sensitivity: Advances in the methodology of grounded theory.* Mill Valley, CA: Sociology Press.

Goulding, C. (1998) Grounded Theory: the missing methodology on the interpretivist agenda. *Qualitative Market Research: An International Journal* 1(1): 50–57.

Hamilton Wood Type Museum (2020) *New impressions: Hello!* Thomas Mayo & Co. Retrieved 24 November 2020, from https://woodtype.org/products/copy-of-new-impressions-hello-thomas-mayo.

Hot Bed Press (2020) *The 20:20 print exchange*. Retrieved 15 November 2020, from https://www.hotbedpress.org/exhibitions/2020-print-exchange/.

International Print Exchange (2020) *International print exchange*. Retrieved 16 November 2020, from https://www.internationalprintexchange.org
Jandrić, P. (2019) Digital: The three ages of the digital. In Ford, Derek R.(ed.) *Keywords in radical philosophy and education* (pp 161–176), Leiden: Brill Sense.
Jury, D. (2004) *Letterpress: The allure of the handmade*. Mies: RotoVision.
Jury, D. (2006) *Letterpress: New applications for traditional skills*. Mies: RotoVision.
Koch, T. (2006) Establishing rigour in qualitative research: the decision trail. *Journal of Advanced Nursing* 53(1): 91–103.
Kühne, D. (2017). *True print/Dafi Kühne*. Zürich: Lars Müller Publishers.
Le Gallais, T. (2008) Where I go there I am: Reflections on reflexivity and the research stance. *Reflective Practice* 9(2): 145–155.
Letterpress Workers (2017) *Edition-2017*. Retrieved 24 November 2020, from https ://letterpressworkers.org/past-events/edition-2017/.
Luckman, S. (2015) Material authenticity and the renaissance of the handmade: The aura of the analogue (or 'the enchantment of making'). In *Craft and the creative economy*. London: Palgrave Macmillan. doi:10.1057/9781137399687_4.
Massumi, B. (2002) *Parables for the virtual. Movement, affect, sensation*. Durham: Duke U.P.
May, T., and Perry, B. (2014) Reflexivity and the practice of qualitative research. In *The SAGE handbook of qualitative data analysis*. London: SAGE Publications Ltd.
Merriam, S. B., and Associates (2002) *Qualitative research in practice*. San Francisco, CA: Jossey-Bass.
Mills, J., Bonner, A., and Francis, K. (2006) The development of constructivist grounded theory. *International Journal of Qualitative Methods* 5(1): 25–35.
Negroponte, N. (1998) Beyond digital. *Wired* 6(12). Retrieved 13 November, from http://www.wired.com/wired/archive/6.12/negroponte.html.
New North Press (2020) *A23D: A 3D-printed letterpress font*. Retrieved 24 November 2020, from http://new-north-press.co.uk/project/a23d/.
Patton, Q. M. (2002) *Qualitative evaluation and research methods* (3rd ed.). Newbury Park, CA: Sage Publication, Inc.
Pepperell, R., and Punt, M. (2000) *The postdigital membrane: Imagination, technology and desire*. Bristol: Intellect.
p98a (2016) *About the gallery*. Retrieved 24 November 2020, from https://www.p98a.com/about.
Rigley, S. (2005) Thinking in solid air. *Eye Magazine* 57: 36–43.
Suzuki, S. (2011) Print people: A brief taxonomy of contemporary printmaking. *Art Journal* 70(4): 6–25.
Strauss, A., and Corbin, J. (1990) *Basics of qualitative research: Grounded theory procedures and techniques*. Newbury Park, CA and London: Sage.
Striano, F. (2019) Towards 'post-digital'. A media theory to re-think the digital revolution. *Ethics in Progress* 10(1): 83–93. doi:10.14746/eip.2019.1.7.
Sundén, J. (2015) Technologies of feeling: Affect between the analog and the digital. In Hillis, K., Paasonen, S., and Petit, M. (Eds.), *Networked affect* (pp 135–149). Cambridge: MIT Press.

Tate (2016) *Anthony Burrill: To the letter – Interview*. Retrieved 16 December 2020, from https://www.tate.org.uk/art/art-terms/p/pop-art/anthony-burrill-letter.

Williamson, C. (2013) *Low-tech: Print contemporary hand-made printing*. London: Laurence King Publishing.

Wilson, C. (2021) *Post-digital printing: The integration of digital technology with contemporary letterpress practice*. Unpublished.

Young, M. M. (2012) *The rise and fall of the printers' international specimen exchange*. New Castle: Oak Knoll Press.

7 Letterpress Experiments in a Design Course

Rita Carvalho

Introduction

With the revitalisation of analogue printing in a post-digital era, risograph and silkscreen publications have been flourishing, as well as independent book fairs (Jury, 2018). Analogue printing workshops have started to return to design studios and courses. It is broadly accepted that this kind of experimentation is relevant in design education, providing what has been often forgotten in recent years, in particular the paradoxical sense of freedom that results from working with the limitations imposed by materials and their physicality.

Although letterpress is part of this context, few undergraduate courses in Portugal have a workshop. This reinforces the need for a debate about the role of letterpress in design education.

This chapter aims to contribute to this discussion by reflecting on the current practices of a letterpress workshop in a BA Hons course in communication design in Lisbon. Three projects – diversified in their aims, processes and results – were analysed, using a literature review and empirical observation, combined with two techniques of biographical-narrative research, in an interpretivist approach.[1]

The Course

Delli (a word that designates both an informal Design Department in the Universidade Lusófona, Lisbon and the studio where workshops and some classes take place) offers an experimental and speculative driven BA Hons course in communication design. Students are encouraged to have a critical attitude towards design and the world – which involves a great deal of discussion and systematic questioning, while also experimenting diversity in terms of references, processes and media.

76 *Rita Carvalho*

Alongside the basics of graphic communication, students start by experimenting analogue technologies, above all expanding their concept of graphic design through an enriching, multi-sensorial approach. Students are introduced to letterpress during the first semester of the course, within the discipline, Colour, Representation and Printing Techniques (CRPT) – taught by myself and Telmo Chaparra – and are provided with further experiences in the context of short courses.

Besides letterpress, students have access in Delli to a digital printer, a RISO machine, silkscreen equipment and some binding-related machinery. There is a close relationship with the production of editorial objects. In fact, exercises developed in classes and workshops often result in printed publications.[2]

The Workshop

The letterpress workshop is recent (as is the course itself) and somewhat modest, requiring some imagination to surpass the scant materials. It has an A3 proofing press and two hand-fed platen presses (these recently acquired) plus a standing-screw press. With regard to type, there are several serif and sans-serif lead and wood alphabets (some of which are complete), from 6 to 480 pt. There are several kinds of spacing materials, which, similarly to chases and quoins, are (sometimes) sufficient.

Until recently, we exclusively used engraving safe-wash ink (oil-based), in order to prevent toxicity in the workshop. The three projects described below were printed using that ink.

We Are the Robots (October 2019)

This song by Kraftwerk set the tone for a group project from the aforementioned first-year discipline (CRPT). There is a retro-futuristic strangeness in the combination of robots and a 500-year-old printing technology, which I hoped could create a good atmosphere for the exercise.

Students (about 20) were asked to craft a typographic illustration depicting a robot in human scale. It had to be printed in two colours,[3] using wood type (optionally articulated with metal engravings) on 37 × 146 cm thin paper. The duration was nine hours (three weekly sessions of three hours each).

This exercise intended to introduce first-year students to the specificities of letterpress, while exploring the expressive potential of the letters themselves, and ultimately, of colour.

The project began with a genealogy of letterpress printing, including an overview of its contemporary uses. A presentation of equipment and materials was followed by a demonstration of the process (composition, printing, stowage and cleaning).

We then observed and commented on a few typographic illustrations in letterpress, found in *Espírito Artes / Espírito Ciência* by Paulo de Cantos (1892–1979); in *Animais Tipográficos* by Ticoolgrafia, or in *Fourth Estate Catalogue* by Frost Design, to mention a few. Besides unveiling some expressive possibilities of this technology (Jury, 2004), this aimed to help students detach the letter from its common function of conveying sound (phonetic writing) in order to access the letter's potential as an expressive shape, capable of producing meaning through a kind of pre-alphabetised logic – i.e. by facing, using and combining it according to its visual/formal similarities to bits of "reality".

However, regressing to that pre-alphabetised mode wasn't automatic or easy. Students were therefore allowed to include one word in the robot's head.

The words were then juxtaposed to form letters, chosen on formal/compositional grounds. After experiencing some difficulties, the students began to play with the letters as pure shapes of an anthropomorphic robot. Despite the playful nature of that typographic "game", there was some despair and complaints, since the time required to build up and close the composition required considerable patience (something to be re-learned by this generation). Nonetheless, the robots' heads were successfully printed in a single colour A3 proofing press.

The same couldn't be achieved with their bodies – which were more than one metre long – which led us to compose and print the bodies on large rectangular tables. A further complication was the shortage of furniture. The students therefore had to make a collective human chain for each composition and hold it up while others carefully placed the paper for the print. The scenario resembled an operation room, and needless to say, there was a great deal of laughter during the process.

In this case we can actually say that the material limitations were partly responsible for the joyful and productive atmosphere, which extends beyond the sense of communion. In fact, the physical effort involved in making the human chain reminded us of one quality of letterpress: as "a valuable counterbalance to that of the sedentary swivel chair" (Jury, 2018, p.172). The benefits of physical activity for art students are immense. Meaghan Barry and Lilian Crum advocate that

> Designing a lifestyle that includes exercise would foster inspiration and break 'creative block', it would promote mental wellness – often an issue within the creative community – and it would also build a strong bond between students to create the best studio environment possible.
> (Barry & Crum, 2018, p. 83)[4]

Although letterpress printing can't be compared to running a marathon, there was considerable physical effort involved.

Scale was a striking point in this project. In combination with the typographic composition, it brought a major impact to the image, which gave students a sense of empowerment.

They recognised the importance of colour in this phenomenon. As the students commented at the end, all the robots displayed highly vibrant colours, where the combination reinforced that boldness, simultaneously endowing a joyful and humorous tone to the pieces.

This first-year project was able to awaken/sharpen a certain graphic designer eye and wit. That was clear in the way that the students composed and then reacted to each other's robots, pointing and laughing at them (that is something which is inherent to typographic illustration: there is nothing but nonsense and humour in a leg defined by a "j" or a mouth by a rotated "d").

Scale played a very positive role in this experience, bringing satisfaction to the production of such a bold image and forcing students to collaborate. Indeed, the strongest contribution of this project for students was to experience the dynamics of letterpress as a collective process — sharing materials, difficulties and efforts. This human dimension is crucial not only to a printing context (Ryder, 1955), but to design-related activities. Unfortunately, the same level of collaboration wasn't always achieved in terms of cleaning and tidying up the workshop. However, that improved over the ensuing weeks.

Praxe. Workshop on Activism (October 2019)

Praxe was a four-day workshop that consisted of creating, printing and implementing a social campaign. It was actually the letterpress component of a larger workshop – *Activism* – which aimed to promote the involvement of students in social matters, as active graphic agents.

The brief established that the general theme was Conflict. After the disclosure and discussion of the work of Corita Kent (1918–1986), Ben Shahn (1898–1969) and Emory Douglas (1943–), among others, the students were divided into four different clusters, corresponding to four distinct means of expression/media: risograph printing; photography; collage; and letterpress.[5]

The letterpress group was responsible for making a set of A3 posters. The students (about 25) could use image or typography only (wood or metal type), or a combination of the two.

After they had been divided into groups, the students observed examples of socially engaged work in this technology by Robin Fior (1935–2021),

Alan Kitching (1940–) and the collective Homem do Saco, followed by comments and a debate, in particular concerning a local political/social issue that would be relevant for the students to work from.

Having decided to work on the theme of *Praxe* (a controversial set of hazing rituals for undergraduates in Portuguese universities), there was a new discussion resulting in slogans for the campaign – some in favour and others against such practices. Indeed, most of the students were against the *Praxe*, because it subjects undergraduates to humiliating practices; but a small group saw those derisive activities as a kind of initiation ritual, that fosters integration in the University. However, they stressed that it is something which participants should be able to reject.

The messages were therefore divided between attacks on the *Praxe*'s mocking practices/practitioners ("I put a potty on my head, how funny am I?") and messages related to free will, such as *"Praxe* is not power, it's a choice".

While one group of students was printing slogans in the proofing press, others stamped their slogans or single key words. By that time, Delli was busy and we could feel a good productive atmosphere.

Some students combined type with images and others used images exclusively. Silhouettes depicting the icons of the *Praxe* – such as the *doutores* (the leaders) or the objects that they use (such as spoons) – were printed through decal, using corrugated cardboard. Curiously, the stripes from the cardboard's texture turned out to be one of the strongest graphic elements, bringing a certain graphic coherence to all the posters.

Finally, students posted their work in the Jardim de Campo Grande in Lisbon – a locus of the *Praxe* and therefore a highly suitable location (Figure 7.1). Students were also fortunate with the platform for hanging the posters, since they used the wooden structures that prop up the young trees. Despite the rain which fell immediately after they affixed their posters, most of the students were enthusiastic, apparently enjoying the illicit nature of the initiative. The final result was confrontational and visually appealing, in a quite raw and unusual manner.

Although there were no signs of interaction between the *doutores* and the posters (which might have confirmed their effectiveness) we can affirm that the students experienced two aspects of letterpress printing:

1. Its ability to autonomously display ideas and beliefs, giving "power to the people", using the expression from the Black Panther Party. It should be added that the irreversibility of printing provided the students with an important experience of responsibility. By inscribing words or images on a piece of paper which was then printed, students had to assume choices, becoming courageously active in society. In a very tangible manner, this marks an alternative to what José Gil (2005)

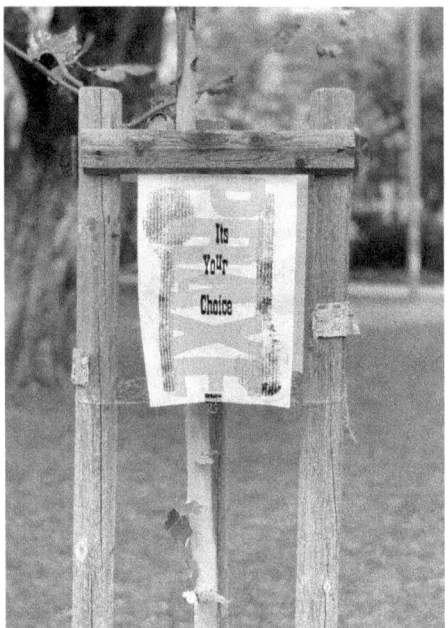

Figure 7.1 Praxe: It's Your Choice. Campo Grande Garden, Oct. 2009. BA Students (Design); José Sebastião (Photo).

describes as the Portuguese phenomena of *non-inscription* – a certain apathy or self-privation of acting towards the things around us (a legacy from a dictatorship that promoted 48 years of quiet resignation[6]).

2. Its adequacy for social issues – a *grafica povera* effect, the feeling of anti-establishment and strong convictions suggested by the imperfections of the graphic object – as Richard Hollis has mentioned, referring to Robin Fior's interventionist work (Hollis, 1999). Indeed, a certain naiveness makes letterpress a privileged medium for expressing a point of view, in particular a political one. Paradoxically, that same naiveness coexists with a kind of solemn quality, a silent dignity, that not only exists in the colourful word on paper but also on the colourless marks of the pressure of the press – a sign of the printer's intention.

Coffee or Taking Type for a Walk (February 2018)

This was an 18-hour workshop in the context of a drawing discipline in the third year of the course. It was the students' first contact with letterpress,

Letterpress Experiments in a Design Course 81

since this workshop took place before the curricular reform that included letterpress as a subject from the first year onwards. Besides introducing students to the technology, it aimed to explore letterpress in combination with drawing, as two expressive resources that don't necessarily pertain to separate universes.

Since the students at the time were exploring the future of coffee – in their main discipline of Design – I decided to choose coffee as a theme as well, in order possibly to provide material for their Design project. However, experimentation was the main goal of this workshop.

We began with a short genealogy of letterpress printing, followed by a demonstration of the several stages of the process. Afterwards, the students (about 20) were divided into four groups and the brief was presented and discussed. They were asked to craft a box containing a set of drawn and printed objects in different formats: a folded leaflet (printed in A3 paper), some A5 cards and a series of 10 × 15 cm postcards. A variety of papers/ cardboard in terms of weight, texture and colour were used. The brief included several texts that alluded to coffee: "Happiness" by Raymond Carver, "The Long Goodbye" by Raymond Chandler, "Black Coffee" by Paul Francis Webster, "Cigarettes and Coffee" by Otis Redding and, lastly, a popular saying by an anonymous author. Students could choose printing parts of one text/lyrics; key words; the author or his social context; or even something else.

Before printing, we went to another room for a couple of hours in order to develop several drawing experiences. At first, students produced a few blind drawings of colleagues drinking coffee, using graphite pencil. The idea was to begin by "taking a line for a walk", to use Paul Klee's expression, allowing them to draw freely in a fluid manner, without the constraints and inhibitions that are inherent to regular observational drawing. In addition, students printed marks on coffee cups and painted abstract marks using coffee as ink and also some dripping. In the end, there was even some time to draw hands holding coffee mugs. The results were then taken into the letterpress workshop and used as a background for some of the prints.

Regarding the suggested texts: apart from one group which chose to print a complete popular saying, the students generally printed a single verse of a song or a few loose words from one of the texts. Others preferred not to use any of the texts, but to print expressions or words about drinking coffee (such as "Wake up!").

In this stage, students had to deal with inadvertently rotated type or inverted words, which caused frustration, but in some cases, satisfaction due to a certain graphic revelation. The lack of type for composing some words induced the same double effect – impatience *versus* joy (in this case for overcoming a problem while attaining a fresh graphic solution).

We only had one proofing press at that time. So, while one group was using it, the other three were doing all kinds of "freestyle" printing with the letterpress material.

The extent and diversity of their experimentation – increased by the wide range of papers – was a pleasant surprise. These students had no previous references, and therefore, no prejudices to limit their actions. As a result, there were a lot of colour experiments with overly inked rollers (which led to beautiful postcards), as some blurry printing generated loose compositions. There was also plenty of stamping, using both type and furniture. One of the students made a very sensitive work on colour and rhythm, by repeating the same letter across the page and subtly varying its position and tone. Others explored a more illustrative approach. There was an image from another student, who stamped a cup (using metal furniture) and the word "steam" emerging from it, evoking visual poetry.

The connection between typographic composition and blind drawing proved to be highly satisfying for the students. Besides the plasticity of the combination, that first drawing layer was able to resolve compositional problems from the typographic layer, by filling empty spaces and thereby assuring a certain unity.

Indeed, the best outcome of this workshop was the recognition, by some students, of drawing as an expressive resource for design, thereby shortening the distance between both, that is frequently felt by students. A sense of freedom and fun resulting from experimenting and combining all this diversity was also very positive.

Conclusions

The above exercises didn't include any digital processes, since we prioritised acknowledgement, by students, of the limitations and potentialities of letterpress. We also believe that one of the most appealing aspects of this technology today (especially for first-year students) is precisely to suspend "reality" by immersing them in an alternative playground that allows the improbable, the absurd and error. The adventure in this "uncharted territory" to use an expression from Suzanna Edwards (2004, p.130) is crucial for opening up minds and fostering creativity.[7]

The experimentation in all three projects made it possible to explore important skills for future communication designers. Not only the basics of graphic communication were addressed (such as colour, composition, typography, drawing), but also a certain graphic humour or wit – in particular, because the process involves having fun.

The ability to work collectively is also an important skill exercised in the Letterpress context, as described above.

So, although some frustration was reported by a few students (resulting either from lack of material or lack of interest), letterpress offers immense benefits for this Design course, transcending visual design issues, since it provides the opportunity to re-learn patience, and also take risks and responsibility, to work with the entire body and to feel the power and joy resulting from having a voice.

Notes

1 Reflections of the researcher and field notes containing records of student reactions in a workshop or class context.
2 Delli has a publishing label – DelliPress – through which these works have been circulating in Portugal and abroad.
3 This was an opportunity to consolidate a theme explored in previous classes – the colour contrasts by Johannes Itten (2004). Indeed, students were asked to produce the contrast of hue.
4 Over the past two years we have encountered several cases of depression and anxiety disorders among our students, whereby exercise is becoming an urgent issue.
5 Coordinated by Luís Alegre, Filipe Luz, António Cruz Rodrigues, João Cunha, David Bota, Marco Balesteros and myself.
6 The *Estado Novo* (1926–1974) was the authoritarian regime in Portugal, led by António de Oliveira Salazar.
7 However, that "uncharted territory" is constantly mutating. We are therefore starting to explore some projects that combine letterpress with digital work, in particular involving laser cutting and risograph.

References

Barry, M., Crum, L. (2018). Teaching a Healthier Creative Process. In B. Smith, L. Monogna, L. S. Turow (Eds.), *Frontier: A Graphic Design Education Reader* (pp 81–86). Bozeman: Montana State University / AIGA.
Edwards, S. (2004). Craft and Education. In D. Jury (Ed.), *Letterpress. The Allure of the Handmade* (pp. 126–139). Mies: Rotovision.
Gil, J. (2005). *Portugal Hoje. O Medo de Existir*. Lisbon: Relógio D'Água.
Hollis, R. (1999). Robin Fior: Revolutionary Language. *Eye Magazine* 32, vol. 8, Summer 1999.
Itten, J. (2004). *Art de la Couleur*. Stuttgart: Dessain et Tolra.
Jury, D. (2004). *Letterpress. The Allure of the Handmade*. Mies: Rotovision.
Jury, D. (2018). *Reinventing Print. Technology and Craft in Typography*. London: Bloomsbury.
Ryder, J. (1955). *Printing for Pleasure*. London: Bodley Head.

Part III
Introduction
Practice

The final part is dedicated to the activities, initiatives and practices in present-day letterpress. It characterises current letterpress as practised by different artists, designers and makers. Since this practice is no longer constrained by commercial activity or production, it is currently being explored in educational or production contexts, mainly in conjunction with other media to restore and nurture traditional practices or even encompassed within hybrid processes to produce richer hybrid communication artefacts.

In Part III we present a sample of approaches—some ground their current methods in the history and revival of techniques and equipment, while others analyse current technologies and incorporate them in the processing of conceptualising and fabricating new digital letterforms. Whether in professional, artistic or educational contexts, all these accounts report a future onlook of the letterform practice, bringing it closer to the individual designer and maker.

The first contribution presents one highlight from the artistic practice of Jorge dos Reis. This is a practice that reflects on a timeless criterion to explore visual and material vicissitudes—such as the material scale, or the white space—of letterpress and how this technology promotes other media expression, such as sound or *performativeness*.

The following chapters address methods and processes that try to bridge both analogue and digital realities into a hybrid process or results. The eighth chapter therefore presents an in-depth characterisation of how several designers and educators are restoring old techniques to produce new type, and how some are hacking common materials and digital tools to recreate and reinterpret letterpress composing and printing processes and materials in present-day education and artistic production.

The ninth chapter provides an insight into the kind of project that takes advantage of currently available technologies in order—building on the shared knowledge of previous makers and DIYers—to design and fabricate a specific letterform that is free from the constraints of existing standardised software tools.

Finally, the tenth chapter describes the similarities and the creative potential aspects of using both functional computer programming and the letterpress printing process to design and generate computer graphics that are intended to be physically printed. By tapping into the rational procedural nature of programming and iterating it with the constraints and expressive nature of the analogue printed medium, the authors, designers and students are able to explore each medium in a symbiotic and very fulfilling manner.

Part III

Practice Highlight: The Rising Letters – Seven Criteria for the Typographic Design of a Letterpress Archive

Proposing a dual, visual and sound analysis, in the extensive survey and registration of the movable type characters in two countries (observed and considered after twenty-five years have passed)

Jorge dos Reis

Introduction

Twenty-five years have passed since the moment when I decided to embark upon a typographic learning path, due to formative and professional needs, by becoming an apprentice of movable type in a composition and printing workshop in the old zone of Lisbon. In the wake of this *stimulus* I had a very personal desire to register, print, and archive the typographic characters that were available in that composing room, producing printed tests on an old, fairly high-quality proofing press, from an ethnographic perspective (Figure P3.1).

The constructive criteria of this archive are twofold: to record all the typographic characters present and explore the sound volume capabilities emanated by each font. Seven criteria are presented herein: (1) the white

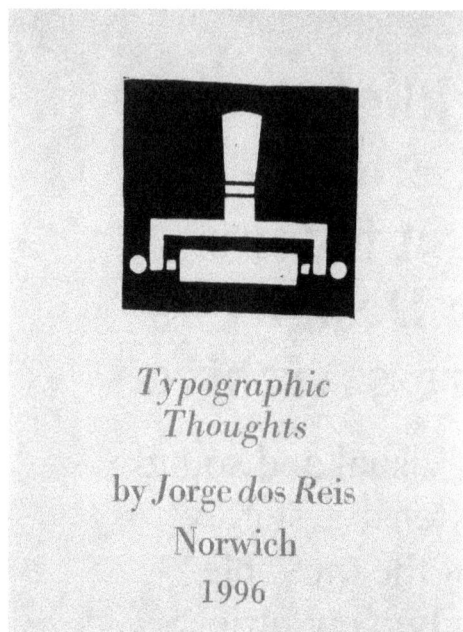

Figure P3.1 Typographic Thoughts. Cover Page of the Norwich Archive, 1996.

space and the typographic scale in the visual area of the page; (2) onomatopoeia, imitation of sounds, and expressive mimicry; (3) the sound approach as a consequence of the transformation of the letterpress piece into a prescribed phonetic performative score; (4) the use of abstract language and its graphic representation; (5) the text reconstruction and wordplay approach; (6) readability and writing in letterpress; (7) orality in the performative discourse present in Schönberg's *Sprechgesang*.

The Seven Criteria for the Construction of the Archive

The criteria that we are going to enunciate herein that constitute the basis for a specific design vision for the construction of a typographic archive, enunciate an individualised practice of typography for the accomplishment of these works or, on the other hand, demonstrate a close connection with the printing houses and spaces where they were carried out.

Each of these seven criteria is based on the fact that it represents its own graphic dimension, a different aesthetic position, in order to consolidate complementary or antagonistic strategies with regard to an understanding of the constructive mechanisms of typographic elements for a typographic archive. Each of them makes personalised use of the materiality of typography, by exploring different methodologies.

Typographic Design Criterion Towards a Letterpress Archive

First Criterion

The white space and the typographic scale in the visual area of the page

In 1895, Lewis Carroll described the tail of a mouse in *Alice in Wonderland*, by typing the end of the paragraph in the shape of a curve, thus creating a visual approximation to the animal described in the story. In addition to this visual and figurative effect, typography can also integrate acoustic qualities, through the way that the message transforms into sound. On the basis of tension and typographic rhythm, the brain composes an acoustic image of the text, as in Stéphane Mallarmé's poem *Un coup de dés jamais n'abolira le hasard*, which evokes auditory and emotional sensations.

Unlike a poem with a conventional format, the text develops inside a visual composition, in which the white space of the page assumes vital importance, since the words are separated, thereby deliberately emphasising the oral expression and emotion of the written message (Drucker, 1994).

Carroll's contribution precedes that of Mallarmé, but it was the latter who transformed the conventional page into a modern page, where the white space is, for the first time, an instrument of work.

Second Criterion

Onomatopoeia, imitation of sounds, and expressive mimicry

Reflecting around Marinetti, it is important to equate how freely expressive typography and spelling make it possible to represent sound values and lyrical aspects. The proportion of characters can express epidermal exuberances, whereas the repetition of individual sounds and letters can form an onomatopoeic score.

In his text about numbers, *Geometric and mechanical splendor and numerical sensitivity*, Marinetti allows us to identify the theoretical assumptions that apply to the performing arts (Kirby, 1971). The onomatopoeic noise brings with it the visualisation of the physical objects:

1) "Direct, imitative, elementary, realistic onomatopoeia" selecting a sequence of sounds that represent reality, just as *ssiiiiii* represents the sound of a towboat's whistle (Apollonio, 2001, p. 158).
2) "Indirect, complex and analog onomatopoeia" alludes to sensations such as weight, heat, colour, smell, and noise, giving us an example of the sound of the sun (Apollonio, 2001, p. 158).
3) "Abstract onomatopoeia" refers to unconscious expressions related to sensitivity. In his poem Dunes, the abstract sound "ran ran ran" simply translates a state of mind (Apollonio, 2001, p. 158).
4) The "psychic onomatopoeia harmony" concerns the fusion of two or three of the onomatopoeias mentioned here (Apollonio, 2001, p. 158).

Third Criterion

The sound approach as a consequence of the transformation of the letterpress piece into a prescribed phonetic performative score

Sound performance is not the declamation of a traditional poem written on paper, even if the declamation is an *oralisation* of a written, experimental, and innovative text in the verbal sounds it presents. The sound performance can indeed resort to a typographic poem that serves as a score, establishing it as the basis of this performative approach. *A posteriori*, sound interpretation becomes a new poem, an autonomous poem. It is possible to recognise the autonomy of the independence of the oral work, resulting from it. But in this strategy, the typographic score is a fundamental reference for the performer.

Hugo Ball performed his poetic performance *Karawane* (Caravan) or *Elefantenkarawane* (Elephant Caravan) on 23 July 1916 at the Cabaret Voltaire in Zurich. In the seventeen lines of this sound poem, Ball used different fonts: italics and roman in lower case, letters with serif and without serif. The artist executed different versions of the poem, changing the typefaces, from which it follows that the movement of the text is directly linked to the richness of these characters (Foster, 2003).

Fourth Criterion

The use of abstract language and its graphic representation

The dynamics of typography on the surface of the page can attract the observer's gaze. By setting the letters free, using various fonts, upper or lower case, and using ultra-thin or ultra-black styles, the Futurists and Dadaists tried to express the different tones of voice and intensity of speech. The optical structure of the printed text gives the audience the ability to hear the mouth sounds, in their full variety. As we have been mentioning, the sensitive and planned typographic arrangements function as sheet music, not only for the performer but also for the audience.

Following this same line of thought, the sound poems of the dadaist typographer Raoul Hausmann were conceived in movable type to be able to manipulate the wooden letters physically and thereby comport abstract words with a strong phonetic component. In an allusion to the sound qualities of the words he had invented, Hausmann named his works letter posters and Phonétique poems, exploring their optical and acoustic dimensions.

In 1918, Hausmann created a set of *optophonetic* poems, *Plakat* and *Optophonetische Gedichte* (Poster and Optophonic Poem), for energetic diction. In the same year, Hausmann produced the poem *Kp'erioum* and another seminal work, *Offeah*, characterised by horizontal lines of upper case and some letters of lower case, in a formally simple composition that had reinforced effect from the acoustic point of view.

Fifth Criterion

The text reconstruction and wordplay approach

The typographic transformation of one text into another, syntactically identical, but with different graphic orientations, where, between the visual spots of the words the white space and the leading are interspersed, is a demanding task for typographic composition. We can find the origin of this approach to text in the wordplay phenomenon.

In the introduction to *Making the Alphabet Dance*, Ross Eckler pays tribute to Dmitri Borgman (the father of wordplay) in the context of the decline of recreational linguistics following the advent of crossword puzzles in 1914 (Eckler, 1997). However, there has been a renewed interest in wordplay over the last 30 years. Eckler goes further and states that this sector of "recreational linguistics that views words as collections of letters to be manipulated is far richer and more subtle than anyone suspected" (Eckler, 1997, p. xi); that may have different applications in the field of typography.

Sixth Criterion

Readability and writing in letterpress

Some of the concerns of graphic mediators are also important for typographic poets who visually work with writing. The decisions imposed on graphic designers, in terms of design, may also be placed on the plane of typography:

- **The size of the page and the number of pages in the book format.** The most important factor, as James Hartley confirms, is to have some knowledge of the form and conditions under which textual information will be used by its users, whether readers or performers (Hartley, 1994, p. 11).
- **The choice of font.** It is common for designers and typographers to use fonts of different sizes. Although there is a consistent relationship between these letter bodies "it is important to note that the choice of this variable is conditioned by previous decisions. Of course, we do not expect to find huge fonts in a dictionary" (Hartley, 1994, p. 31).
- **The structure and the white space.** This particular aspect affects visual comfort and the way in which the reader or interpreter will appropriate the typographic message; the space that is between letters and words, the leading and the white margins.

Seventh Criterion

Orality in the performative discourse present in Schönberg's Sprechgesang

Another important aspect for the approach of typography in performative practice and for its phonetic interpretation is Schönberg's vocal technique: *Sprechgesang* which in German means singing-speech or spoken singing, or *Fstimme* – voice-to-speech or spoken voice. This technique is located halfway between singing and speaking and was used by this composer of the second school of Vienna in his work *Pierrot Lunaire* (1912).

The mediation between speech and singing, present in the *Sprechgesang*, is also detectable in the work of certain typographers who resorted to orality in order to prolong their typographic poem phonetically.

The syllable organisation of the *Sprechstimme* of this composition, the techniques of musical contrast, and the relationship between words constitute strong compositional elements.

Conclusion

In terms of conclusion, we can mention that many graphic designers and typographers in the field of letterpress use these criteria intuitively in their work to give more expression to the text, certainly without an objective, prescribed, and perceptible awareness. Its use is justified in view of the reason that when looking at this archive (which is then revealed in some of its constituents) many authors of graphic design and typography will look in the mirror whenever they want to confront the alphabetical sounds of their graphic design projects and thereby overcome the coldness of printed typography.

References

Apollonio, U. (2001). *Futurist Manifestos*. Boston: MFA Publications.
Drucker, J. (1994). *The Visible Word, Experimental Typography and Modern Art, 1909–1923*. Chicago: The University of Chicago Press.
Eckler, R. (1997). *Making the Alphabet Dance*. London: Macmillan.
Foster, H. (2003). "Dada Mime" in *October No. 105*. Boston: MIT Press.
Hartley, J. (1994) *Designing Instructional Text*. London: Kogan Page.
Kirby, M. (1971). *Futurist Performance*. New York: PAJ Publications.

8 Digital Fabrication

Expanding Access to and Preservation of Letterpress Printing

Erin Beckloff

Letterpress is a manual, mechanical and technical process of relief printing with moveable type and printing presses. Since its inception more than 550 years ago, manufacturing technology has been an inherent part of the printing process. Once an essential means of communication, letterpress has reemerged over recent decades as a technology of craft, art and design (Raffaelli, 2019). Professional and amateur printers and craftspersons have formed a multigenerational community dedicated to sharing knowledge for the use and preservation of letterpress.

Traditional handset type, antique printing presses and equipment remain dominant elements of the letterpress process. In the mid-twentieth century, printing was ranked as the fourth largest industry in the United States (Holmes, 1947). Centuries' worth of mass-produced letterpress equipment and materials were ultimately replaced in the late 1960s by offset printing, leaving a large quantity of unused historical cast iron and steel printing presses, as well as fonts of wood and metal type, waiting to be revitalised by printers. As letterpress has grown in popularity as a form of personal expression, access to presses and type has decreased and demand is driving costs higher, creating barriers to entry to the craft. With this transition from industrial production to individual printers, a need has developed to acquire or produce more presses and printing materials, in particular smaller, lighter and less expensive options.

Over the last 15 years, "digital fabrication" has become an integral part of the technological evolution of letterpress printing. This term refers to processes that use computer-controlled tools to produce physical materials (Gershenfeld, 2012). Throughout the history of letterpress, craftspersons with specialised skills have used the tools of their epoch to increase printing productivity and efficiency. Today, letterpress craftspersons have adopted the use of digital fabrication tools—predominantly the subtractive manufacturing processes of laser cutting and CNC milling—to create a new wood type, printing materials and presses.

Qualitative analysis of interviews conducted in 2020 with leading American letterpress designers and craftsmen, Brad Vetter, Scott Moore, Ryan Molloy and Steve Garst reveal similar motivations and philosophies for using digital fabrication in their work. Their knowledge developed through a combination of their prior experience, inspiration from printing history, access to machinery through makerspaces, and the willingness to learn from and share new manufacturing technology with others. Digital fabrication tools are helping expand accessibility to materials and equipment, which increases the enriched growth and preservation of letterpress printing in both education and practice.

The Evolution of Printing and Manufacturing Technology

Technological development was driven by craftsmen working in the context of their respective epoch, applying their prior experience and specialised knowledge to invent machinery that drove both industrial printing and societal progress. The invention of moveable type, circa 1455, impacted the cognitive development of humankind, influenced culture, and transformed society. The fifteenth-century father of printing, Johannes Gutenberg, applied his knowledge of metals, attained as a master goldsmith and guild member in Mainz, Germany (Christie, 2015), to the traditional manufacturing process of casting. Gutenberg created the process for hand casting "separate reusable metal characters" with molten type metal, hand moulds, and interchangeable letter dies (called matrices) —"the only 'viable' method for making type for three-hundred fifty years" (Nelson et al., 2020, pp. 3–11).

Rapid growth and increased demands for printing on an industrial scale led to the development of automated type manufacturing machinery, driven by American craftsmen at the turn of the twentieth century. In 1834, William Leavenworth introduced the pantograph, a parallelogram-based instrument for duplicating a shape to a reduced or enlarged scale (Encyclopaedia Britannica), which he combined with Darius Wells' router system (in 1826). This combination formed the basic machinery required for making wood type on a production basis. (Shields, n.d.) Nineteenth-century printer David Bruce Jr. worked in his father's type foundry and, by referencing hand casting, he invented the first mechanical process for making metal type—the pivotal typecaster—in 1838 (Nelson et al., 2020). Manufacturing processes of casting and routing were vital to the advancement of printing.

Throughout the evolution of printing technology, craftsmanship has been fundamental to both the practice and manufacturing aspects of letterpress. In her book *The Lost World of the Craft Printer,* Maggie Holtzberg-Call interviews and interprets the stories of commercial printers. One journeyman printer interviewed describes the craft process as a combination of skill, patience, control, and pride in workmanship. "Craftsmanship was common, the tradition in the early 20th century," she writes (Holtzberg-Call, 1992, p. 20). A significant change occurred in the printing industry with the creation of the computer; Holtzberg-Call describes this dramatic shift as a move from visible forces to invisible forces, from mechanical to electronic. While letterpress neared commercial obsolescence and saw a rapid decline in mass production, a rejuvenation of the craft occurred, paralleling the digital fabrication and maker movements. "What proved to be most influential in the expansion of letterpress work after 1985 was the expressive territory opened up by computer technology" (Bright, 2011, p. 135). A new generation of printers guided letterpress into the disciplines of craft, art, and design, creating expressive and functional work ranging from social stationery, wedding invitations, and artist books to fine prints and posters. For hundreds of years, technological development has shaped and reshaped the "narrative environment peculiar to the printing trade" (Holtzberg-Call, 1992, p. 3) and is part of the body of knowledge that craftspersons are applying to the use of digital fabrication tools.

Traditional, or conventional, manufacturing includes subtractive, formative and joining processes (Conner et al., 2014). Printing technology evolved in tandem with traditional manufacturing and has made a seamless connection to the latest manufacturing advancements through digital fabrication. The roots of the digital fabrication movement "date back to 1952, when researchers at the Massachusetts Institute of Technology (MIT) wired an early digital computer to a milling machine, creating the first numerically controlled machine tool" (Gershenfeld, 2012, p. 43). Today, MIT's Center for Bits and Atoms (CBA) is a laboratory that breaks down boundaries between the digital and physical worlds (Gershenfeld, n.d.). The CBA created fab labs (2001), shorthand for "fabrication labs" or "fabulous labs," which "form part of a larger 'maker movement' of high-tech do-it-yourselfers, who are democratizing access to the modern means to make things" (Gershenfeld, 2012, p. 47). Fab labs, as well as makerspaces in educational institutions and community centres, provide open access to a range of high- and low-tech tools, including digital fabrication methods such as computer numerical control (CNC) machines, laser cutters, and 3D printers. 3D printers use additive manufacturing, a technique in which a part is made by depositing material layer-by-layer rather than material being removed (Conner et al., 2014). Pioneering the use of digital fabrication for letterpress manufacturing, Vetter, Moore, Molloy and Garst were all introduced to the technology and tools at community or educational makerspaces. Makerspaces and the contemporary letterpress community have parallel goals of making technologies and knowledge available without restrictions.

As letterpress shifted from an industrial to an individual scale, in tandem with the rise of the personal computer, designers and artists began to integrate digital design with physical printing. Access to design software increased and extensive quantities of fonts of digital type became widely available. Digital fabrication tools rely on plans being inputted from software to produce a physical product. The plans are produced using design software such as Adobe Illustrator, which creates vector-based files that work directly with laser cutters and can automate cutting paths for CNC machines. With design software directly communicating with the tools, rather than needing complex code, digital fabrication has become more accessible and easier to use.

Pioneering the Use of Digital Fabrication for Letterpress Manufacturing

For Brad Vetter, the laser cutter has become an integrated tool in his creative process (B. Vetter, personal communication, December 9, 2020). As a freelance designer and printer, he produces commercial and large-scale letterpress work for musicians, distilleries, restaurants, and a range of other clients. Vetter's career in letterpress began at Hatch Show Print, a 140-year-old poster shop, and icon of American letterpress. His foundation revolved around having an expansive collection of wood type, metal type, and woodcuts from 1880 with which to create gig posters. When he stepped away from Hatch, he found himself with minimal printing materials and a single press. Access to a laser cutter at Northern Illinois University's School of Art and Design became formative to the development of his own style. Instead of recontextualising historic elements as he did at Hatch, he could laser cut an entire poster "that was celebrating the aesthetics and the history of letterpress," but also allowed him to create something that felt original.

Vetter works with colour, line, pattern, and type, embracing the "things that make letterpress innately beautiful." His goal is for those four elements to be perfect, with the only aesthetic imperfections coming from the printing quality. Perfection can be controlled through the use of the laser cutter to engrave or cut printing plates of his digitally designed imagery into inexpensive birch veneer plywood. Vetter explains, "I always start in the composing room, I'm still typesetting and printing every word that will then be laser cut so that I'm celebrating the scratches and dents of antique wood type." He also exploits some of the imperfections of what would technically be considered "poor printing" with the proofs he prints and scans in order to emulate the "letterpress aesthetic." Vetter believes manipulation of the cutting process adds to the aesthetic and opens up design possibilities. The limitations of letterpress, including the materials and time involved, combined with the laser cutter as an embedded tool in his collection, have presented themselves as opportunities for Vetter to innovate, learn and print in ways he had never done before.

Wood type has gained popularity with the new generation of letterpress printers, yet the scarcity of fonts has driven up prices, and desirable decorative ornaments and borders, in particular, are rare. With the early nineteenth-century expansion of printing in America, there was a need for large, cheaply produced letters for use on broadsides or posters. "Wood was the logical material because of its lightness, availability, and known printing qualities" (Shields, n.d.), and it also proved to be exceptionally durable: a vast majority of wood type in use today was produced during that period. Due to renewed demand for wood type in the early 2000s, which has increased ever since, Virgin Wood Type Manufacturing Company (USA), Petrescu Press (Romania), McKellier Woodtype (UK) and Moore Wood Type (USA) have dedicated themselves to the craft and distribution thereof.

Scott Moore established Moore Wood Type after retiring from teaching high school industrial arts for 35 years (S. Moore, personal communication, December 7, 2020). He makes historic revivals of wood type ornaments, fancy dashes, catchwords, and replacement letters for fonts using both pantograph and laser-cutting techniques. The first step in creating wood type is the time-intensive preparation of end-grain maple slabs to "type high." Moore learned most of the process for preparing maple and cutting type through mentorship with Norb Brylski, a former Hamilton Manufacturing Company employee. On a visit to what is now the Hamilton Wood Type & Printing Museum, he studied the original type manufacturing machinery and saw similarities to smaller equivalents in current machinery. Moore's pantograph was created by modifying a metal engraving machine. To use a wood type pantograph, a dimensional pattern of the design is traced while the router replicates the pattern, cutting it into the prepared maple block.

Initially, Moore drew his patterns as vector art and cut them out using woodworking and hand tools. To improve his skills, he attended a workshop at a makerspace, where he learned to make patterns on the laser cutter. Beyond cutting patterns, Moore realised that he could engrave directly into the end-grain maple to produce type with the laser cutter—a process that he now uses for 90% of his type production. The wood type still has to be cut to size from slabs with a trim saw, but the laser cutter revolutionised the scale at which he could make type. Moore explained that the pantograph is faster for clearing away material and ideal for large wood type but that he can make much smaller, more detailed versions with great accuracy using the laser cutter. Harnessing digital fabrication fulfilled a need for people that have tabletop platen or proof presses and can only print with smaller wood type.

Ryan Molloy is an interdisciplinary designer and educator currently teaching graphic design at Eastern Michigan University (R. Molloy, personal communication, December 18, 2020). When he reconnected with letterpress many years after using it in graduate school, he did a survey of existing wood type manufacturing in the hope of making his own experimental type. Driven by his personal curiosity and comfort with emerging technologies, he built a CNC machine, which he describes as "the computerized cousin of the pantograph." Molloy began by analysing the fabrication of Nesbitt "Roman Grotesque," an ornate font with the letters bent horizontally into a V-shape at their centres. Working only from the printed 1838 Nesbitt type specimen book, he decided to recreate the font using the CNC to carve the forms of the actual block, allowing the angular letters to kern, or nest, next to each other, in a line. The majority of wood type is cut on a rectangular block or body. Molloy uses CNC milling to investigate unusual shapes of blocks. His contemporary designs of fonts and ornaments are informed by typographic history and the "native language of the machine and aesthetic that only belongs to the CNC."

Educator and artist Steve Garst created the Provisional Press, a digitally fabricated portable proof press (S. Garst, personal communication, December 16, 2020). The wooden cylinder press can be cut with open-source plans from a single sheet of plywood on a laser cutter and assembled with minimal tools or building experience. After studying printmaking in college and teaching, he was determined to find ways to make the arts accessible, specifically in terms of cost and access to equipment. Garst reverse-engineered the Provisional Press from his 100-year-old steel Nolan Proofing Press. He took inspiration for his design from the Nolan because of his familiarity with it and the simplicity of the printing mechanism.

In 2020, the Provisional Press became a significant solution for remote or socially distanced face-to-face teaching during the COVID-19 pandemic. Garst, with the help of Scott Moore, revised his plans to be a mass-produced kit of parts to meet the expressed needs of college and university educators: accessibility and adaptability for the continuity of letterpress education. Schools provided the press kits to be assembled remotely or checked out, combined with new or historic printing materials, and used by students to retain the quality of learning. By January 2021, Garst had produced 400 kits and additional schools had used his open-source plans to produce their own presses.

Because "relief and letterpress printing are planographic processes," Garst believes laser cutters are an appropriate tool for making the open-source press. With both the original open-source Provisional Press plans and kits, Garst was able to design an affordable printing press out of easily sourced, high-quality parts due to increased access to digital fabrication tools through schools, makerspaces, and personal acquisition.

Securing the Future of Letterpress through Collaboration and Accessibility

Like Gutenberg and Bruce before them, each craftsperson had prior experiences that informed their use of manufacturing technology, choosing digital fabrication tools to create their historically inspired letterpress work. Vetter's eight years of printing over 600 poster jobs at Hatch has allowed him to translate his knowledge to manipulate the laser cutter to produce his imagery with an authentic letterpress aesthetic. Moore combines old technologies he knows from forty years of building wooden furniture and children's toys and hand engraving metal to make an accurate wood type. Molloy's undergraduate and professional background in architecture introduced him to woodworking and digital fabrication methods. Having been raised on a farm, Garst learned economic ways to make and fix things that would withstand the forces of use.

Historically, printers and craftspersons had to conceal their techniques to maintain a competitive advantage in the industry: "Secrecy in the printing trade continued even into the twentieth century. Printers were very reluctant to share their craft with anyone, especially others who might, in some way, be a potential threat to their job security" (Nelson et al., 2020, p. 13). The shift from a trade to existing within craft, art and design paralleled the resurgence of hand making and the DIY movement, simultaneously preserving letterpress. The competition of the past has been replaced by online communication within the letterpress community and active promotion of shared co-construction experiences—demonstrated by the way that Vetter, Moore, Molloy and Garst openly share their knowledge. They all teach their digital fabrication techniques through community, conference, and university workshops. They provide information about their techniques to the public through websites and social media. Moore, Molloy and the wood type community experiment and share what they discover. Vetter and Molloy want to see how other people use their ideas with laser cutting and CNC milling, which will then inform the evolution of their processes. As an open-source project, Garst hopes the Provisional Press will be made and improved through collective experimentation and discussion (Figure 8.1).

The use of digital fabrication tools is both evolving and adding to the visual identity of letterpress by introducing new materials, textures, sizes and design elements for printing. Access to digital fabrication tools via makerspaces, the letterpress community and art centres are, as Garst suggests, contributing to the "evolving nature of being a maker in the twenty-first century." Individuals who are grounded in the fundamentals of the discipline and historical principles of printing share their skill and pride in

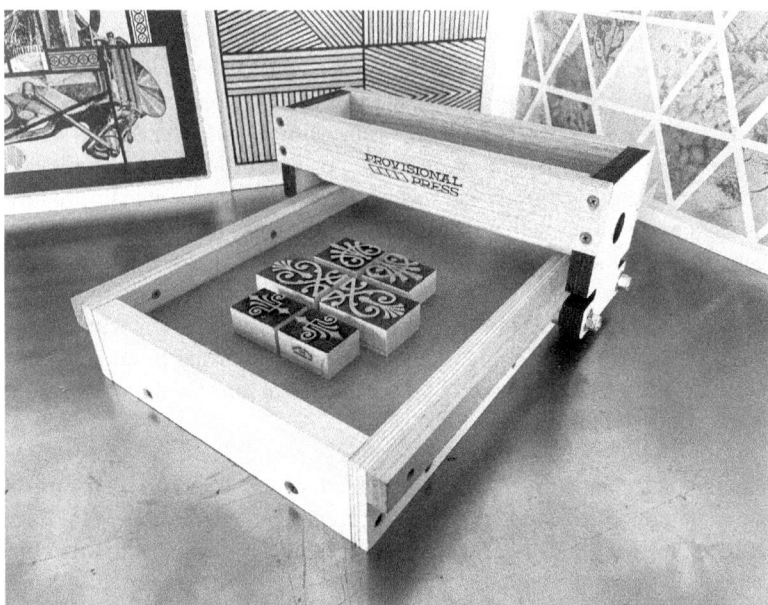

Figure 8.1 Provisional Press Designed by Steve Garst with Wood Type Created by Scott Moore of Moore Wood Type and Posters by Brad Vetter.

craftsmanship through their products and process. Accessibility to letterpress printing equipment, materials and knowledge will continue to expand, allowing the craft to grow through the use of digital fabrication in education and practice.

References

Bright, B. (2011). Handwork and hybrids: Recasting the craft of letterpress printing. In M. E. Buszek (Ed.), *Extra/ordinary: Craft and contemporary art* (pp 135–152). Durham: Duke University Press.

Christie, A. (2015). *Gutenberg's apprentice: A novel*. New York: HarperCollins Publishers.

Conner, B. P., G. P. Manogharan, A. N. Martof, L. M. Rodomsky, C. M. Rodomsky, D. C. Jordan, J. W. Limperos. (2014). Making sense of 3-D printing: Creating a map of additive manufacturing products and services. Additive Manufacturing, 1–4: 64–76.

Encyclopaedia britannica: Pantograph. Retrieved 2021-01-23 from https://www.britannica.com/art/pantograph

Gershenfeld, N. (2012). How to make almost anything: The digital fabrication revolution. *Foreign Affairs*, 91(6): 43–57.

Gershenfeld, N. (n.d.) Prof. Neil Gershenfeld biography. Retrieved 2021-01-06 from http://ng.cba.mit.edu/neil/bio/

Holmes (Burton) Films, Inc. (1947). Printing: Vocational Guidance Films, Inc. Retrieved 2021-01-24 from http://blog.archive.org/2007/07/09/your-life-work/

Holtzberg-Call, M. (1992). *The lost world of the craft printer*. Urbana; Chicago: University of Illinois Press.

Nelson, R. S., S. O. Saxe, D. M. MacMillan, R. L. Hopkins. (2020). *Making printer's type: Man's 500 year quest to develop better methods*. Terra Alta: Hill & Dale Private Press and Typefoundry.

Raffaelli, R. (2019). Technology reemergence: Creating new value for old technologies in swiss mechanical watchmaking, 1970–2008. *Administrative Science Quarterly*, 64(3): 576–618.

Shields, D. (n.d.) What is wood type? Retrieved 2021-01-22 from https://woodtype.org/pages/what-is-wood-type

9 Resisting Hyper-Digitalisation
Investigating Hybrid Practices in Contemporary Graphic Design

Lucrezia Russo

Introduction

Over the last two decades, the exponential development of technology has impacted all creative practices and has radically changed graphic design perspectives. Companies such as Apple, Adobe, or Google have been the driving force behind this change, providing easy access to computers, computer interfaces, and design tools in the attempt to democratise creativity and design culture. Promoting what they claimed to be universal and definitive principles of design (Google Design, 2015), these companies have, instead, flattened design aesthetics and fostered the commodification of design production, rather than its democratisation.

With the release of *Processing* in 2001, Casey Reas and Ben Fry proposed an easy-to-use, accessible coding language and programming environment dedicated to artists and designers to sketch new ideas (CAST Symposium, 2017). The core idea of *Processing* was to provide an educational tool for learning the principles of graphic design, such as colour and composition, "through the medium of computation"(CAST Symposium, 2017). Their proposition took inspiration from the open-source model and promoted the idea of "learning to create software" as opposed to "learning to use software," which, in their opinion, marked a critical point of the crisis of design methodologies in the late 1990s (CAST Symposium, 2017). The auto-productive methods, historically related exclusively to software development, entered into the field of graphic design and design education, and *Processing* was quickly adopted by professionals who embraced its potential as a modular, expandable, and customisable kit (CAST Symposium, 2017).

The customisation of design tools proposed by Casey Reas and Ben Fry was a response to the commodification of design induced by tech companies, and *Processing* proved how programming could provide new perspectives, through the development of a contemporary craft, not only to

DOI: 10.4324/9781003173113-15

expand creativity but to combat the normalisation of design imposed by design monopoles.

Inspired by the open-source and hacker cultures, contemporary graphic designers and graphic design studios have since embraced these unorthodox processes and, through the self-production of devices, have developed hybrid practices that mix analogue, digital, and computational tools.

This new direction in graphic design production seems to be critical. After decades of staring at screens and claiming the death of paper and printing, the rise of these unconventional practices has revealed how new technologies can improve graphic design aesthetics and generate new opportunities for traditional, and sometimes obsolete, printing methods. Do It Yourself (DIY), open-source, and hacker cultures are actively providing valid methodologies to achieve this improvement. Today, we are witnessing the conception of community and spaces built around objects of creation, such as a RISO duplicator or a letterpress press, that are placed next to laser cutters, plotters, and 3D printers. *Hacking* – in its more contemporary meaning of "ingenious combination, or invention" (Triclot, 2011) – is crucial and provides relevant experimentations intersecting new technologies with traditional techniques. This unorthodox attitude embraces the lessons taught by *Processing* and, additionally, restores the role of computers as tools that serve the design practice, instead of controlling the practice itself. Therefore, compelling combinations of realms, previously considered to be in opposition, are blooming and altering the aesthetics of graphic design.

In this context, this research will investigate how the Do It Yourself (DIY), open-source, and hacker cultures have inspired new methodologies for the visual arts, and, in turn, how digital fabrication can progress the practice of traditional printing techniques within the context of contemporary graphic design. To this end, there will be a discussion on how this approach could exist within the framework of formal Art and Design institutions and, considering their limitations of materials, equipment, and space, how digital fabrication may improve the pedagogical approaches to graphic design.

The Impact of Digital Fabrication on Traditional Printing Practices

In investigating the crossing of analogue and digital processes, two patterns have emerged as the most relevant in contemporary design practice, both aiming to emancipate from normalisation and commodification of aesthetics.

The community that has grown up around *Processing* and creative coding has pursued its mission of developing easy-to-use digital tools, providing alternative software or platform for the visual arts. The respective work is often focused on building interactive devices and installations, frequently on the frontier between art and design practices. The connection between creative coding and printing has been translated primarily into the development of libraries that help transfer the generated drawings to paper: their productions primarily employ and manipulate RISO duplicators, drawing machines, such as pen-plotters, and, eventually, obsolete machines, hacked to add materiality to code-generated patterns. The results of these explorations are still facing issues of resolution and scale but are leading to fascinating processes. Julien Gachadoat (V3ga) and Louis Eveillard's experimentations with their hacked embroidery machine *Tricodeur* (Gachadoat, 2014), or Licia He's generated pen-plotted paintings (He, n.d.) prove that young generations of artists and designers are susceptible to these opportunities and, with no inhibitions, are dismantling the traditional separation between the virtual space of screens and the material space of studios.

If the emerging models connected to the realm of creative coding are growing in a territory that intersects art and design, digital fabrication played a critical role in developing the professional graphic design practice, relying on DIY methodologies of auto-production of tools from a professional production standpoint.

Digital fabrication processes—intended as laser cutting and 3D-printing techniques—have successfully contributed to giving new perspectives to traditional printing methods, and in particular to letterpress. Since the mid-2010s, printers and designers have explored new production territories to expand their typefaces collections for letterpress printing. In 2016, the Berlin-based experimental letterpress workshop, a98p, had "tried it all: plexi, maple, pear, resin, magnesium, polymer, formica. CNC milling, 3D-printing, pantograph cutting, etched metal, vacuum-forming" (p98a, 2016). Between 2014 and 2017, the London-based letterpress printer and design studio, New North Press, developed compelling experimentations, such as the 3D-printed typeface A23D or the laser-cut hexagonal woodblocks system AHP Six. Both projects aimed to capitalise on new technologies to empower professional productions in traditional printing (New North Press, 2014).

Over recent years, the development of affordable and valid desktop laser cutters and 3D printers has pushed the boundaries of graphic experimentation even further, enabling a disinhibited typographical approach, defying classical typesetting canons.

The work of printers and designers such as the British designer, Thomas Mayo, or the American Ryan Molloy are examples of how digital fabrication, in particular laser cutting, has been organically implemented in the graphic design practice as an active part of the design process.

Digital fabrication may be legitimately considered to be one of the most critical advancements for letterpress since the adoption of photopolymer plates in the 1980s and has contributed to expanding the community of designers around it, providing a renewal of tradition and the development of a new craft in opposition to the over-digitised contemporary design productions.

Open-Source Sharing Model and the New Craft

In the context of this new craft, some cases have proven how the open-source model of free exchange and collaboration, conventionally considered for software development, could also be relevant in fields such as traditional printing.

In 2018, Martin Schneider and Dominik Schmitz published the plans of The Open Press Project, a "tiny 3D-printed etching press that will let you use these [printing] techniques outdoors, in your living room or small studio" (Open Press Project, n.d.). The two designers from Cologne, Germany, aware of the challenge of accessing an etching press, "wanted to give more people the option to use them for their art in places where printmaking was not possible before." The project received extraordinary support, and a community proliferated around it, proving the relevance of enabling easy access to printing tools.

This model of free exchange of knowledge for creating printing opportunities bloomed during the global health crisis in 2020. During the COVID-19 pandemic, The Provisional Press, portable letterpress, proved the relevance of implementing DIY methodologies to create affordable tools to foster online teaching. Considering students' financial and space restrictions, Steve Garst and his wife Liz, with the help of Scott Moore of Moore Wood Type, designed and provided a kit that could "be built by someone with little woodshop skills but access to a laser cutter" (Provisional Press, n.d.a). This press could "provide an inexpensive alternative that [could] act as a transitional press to enable students to make prints when they may not have access to a large steel press." All plans and instructions are available online and, faithful to the open-source free-exchange spirit, "free for anyone to use and modify as they experiment with building their own press" (Provisional Press, n.d.b).

These ideas resonate with the "modular, expandable, and customisable kit" (CAST Symposium, 2017) proposed by Casey Reas and Ben Fry with *Processing,* and have been transferred from digital to analogue, from screen to print.

The auto-productive and auto-didactic approach inspired by the open-source sharing model and DIY methodology is relevant if we think about fostering access to education outside the educational institutions, growing new territories for the design practice, and expanding creative processes.

Nevertheless, if we think about financial or space limitations within the institutions themselves, how could these methodologies inspire new pedagogical perspectives and help shape the next generation of professionals? Furthermore, using these limitations as a creative resource, could we prepare the next designers to think critically about their practice, their tools, and new technological opportunities, capitalising on constraints, imperfections, and hybridisation?

Launched in 2019, the project *Mobile Uno* is the first attempt to investigate these questions.

Mobile Uno

In 2014, Richard Ardagh of New North Press commissioned a 3D-printed letterpress font from Scott Williams and Henrik Kubel of the foundry A2-Type. The font was a prototype merging the newest digital fabrication and traditional printing techniques, and the typeface A23D results from that experiment (New North Press, 2014). Modelled by Chalk Studios and produced with the finest and most advanced processes at the time, A23D is still considered to be one of the most relevant examples of the intersection between 3D printing and traditional printing techniques.

Inspired by A23D, the project *Mobile Uno* was developed to investigate contemporary intersections between graphic design and digital fabrication. Merging typography, 3D printing, and traditional printing methods seemed an ideal opportunity to advance research into hybrid practices and the crossing of analogue and digital tools. Furthermore, the research aimed to develop alternative creative processes to empower not only graphic design but also the associated pedagogical approaches.

Aware of the limitations of equipment and materials within the educational institutions, how does digital fabrication contribute to improving graphic design pedagogy and shape future professionals? The experiment of A23D aimed to merge digital and analogue approaches in the frame of professional practice, resulting in high-quality objects reliant on the efforts of design and production specialists (Harrison, 2014). Rather than aspire to achieve perfection, *Mobile Uno* wanted to capitalise on the process's limitations and imperfections and use them as a creative resource, adopting a contemporary approach built on hacker and DIY cultures, shown to be critically relevant by The Provisional Press or The Open Press Project.

The *Mobile Uno* alphabet was initially designed in two dimensions in the early 2000s and was part of the ongoing project "Architectural

Types," an exploration of typography and architectural space's interconnections. Alongside *Mobile Uno*, two other sets of letters, *Olympiades* and *Quartopiano*, emerged from intersecting the two-dimensional and three-dimensional spaces. Drawing inspiration from brutalist building and perspective, the intention was to use these alternative typefaces as components of more complex design projects, such as identities or books.

This new alphabet was the central element of the identity designed to communicate a series of furniture elements. The pieces of furniture were conceived respecting the proportions of the *Modulor*, a unit of measurement developed by Le Corbusier in the late 1940s: the letters of *Mobile Uno* also respect these proportions. Adding a third dimension to the alphabet and creating tangible and concrete artefacts provided the opportunity to expand the original project in a direction that was faithful to its origins.

The first step of the project was to create 3D-printed artefacts that would become printing tools. After importing the two-dimensional drawings in a 3D modelling software, the letters were extruded and 3D-printed, with different thicknesses, heights, and sizes (Figure 9.1, top left). The first printing prototypes were used to test the ink's adherence, the artefacts' resistance to pressure, and evaluate the aesthetics of the outcomes (Figure 9.1, top right). It was evident that the pieces created with a desktop 3D printer were fragile and required adjustments, in terms of proportions and density, to support the pressure of a press.

At this stage, it is important to clarify that the artefacts were intended to become printing tools similar to letterpress blocks. Nevertheless, the institution where the research has been conducted did not (and still does not) have a letterpress workshop. Part of the experiment was to build a letterpress-kind-of-process to be adopted in the printmaking workshop to teach students different printing techniques and processes, despite the limitations of the facilities. The first printing tests have been developed with an etching press, simulating letterpress typographical compositions using a cardboard laser-cut frame.

Despite the fragility of the pieces, the printing tests' outcomes delivered an intriguing result: the traces left by the letters were textured, revealing the materiality inherent to the artefacts' imperfections (Figure 9.1, top right). Interestingly, embracing the desktop 3D printer's flaw, we obtained a compelling effect that would not exist without the machine's limitations.

The artefacts were then modified to resist the pressure, but nothing was done to avoid the surface imperfections, which became part of the intrinsic strength of the 3D-printed pieces. The final prototype resulted in nine letters, composing the words "mobile uno" framed in one squared cardboard support, used to assist the pressing process (Figure 9.1, bottom).

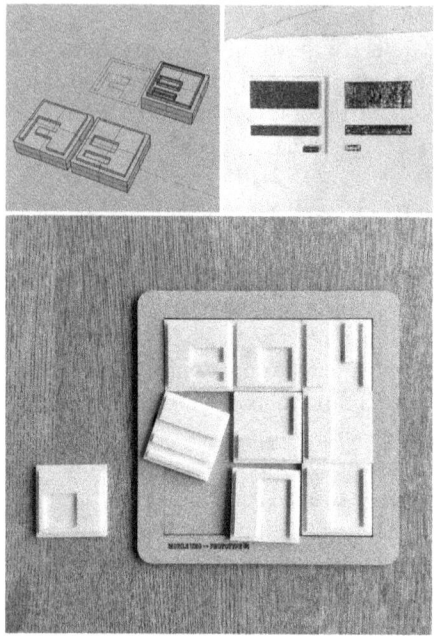

Figure 9.1 Mobile Uno: 3D Model (Top Left), Printing Test Results (Top Right), and Physical Prototype (Bottom).

Investigating the potential of other facilities within the institution was the next step of this research. Using acrylic plastic sheets and drawing inspiration from old-fashioned plastic letter stencils, a set of stencil prototypes was designed and produced with the desktop laser cut to extend the tools to be used in the printing room. Some stickers used as masks on silkscreen frames were also cut out in the school's Fab Lab.

The project *Mobile Uno* is still ongoing and has been placed temporarily on hold due to the current global health crisis. Experimentations to date include 3D-printed letterpress characters, laser-cut letter stencils in Plexiglass, mono-print tiles that pare laser-cut and 3D-printed elements to compare materials, laser-cut modular tiles for custom mono-prints or embossing, and plotted masks for silk screen frames. The project intends to generate a catalogue of tools and instructions to expand traditional printmaking and educational resources, using affordable facilities and techniques through the prototyping process. Inspired by the DIY and hacker cultures, this approach constitutes an invitation to improve working, teaching, and learning techniques through auto-didactic and auto-productive practices.

Conclusion

During the last two decades, graphic design production has been profoundly impacted by high-speed technological advancements, and giant tech companies have contributed, through monopolisation of the digital tools' offer, to standardisation of graphic design aesthetics. In reaction to the design culture's commodification induced by these patterns, unconventional and compelling approaches have emerged, offering new perspectives on graphic design practice.

Drawing inspiration from the open-source and Do It Yourself (DIY) cultures, artists and designers have implemented self-made tools and auto-productive approaches, shifting their practices towards a new craft, reacting to the standardisation of aesthetics and the hyper-digitalisation that have marked the design field since the late 1990s. Hybrid practices, relying on the combination of analogue, digital, and computational tools, have bloomed, restoring the role of computers as tools that serve the design practice instead of controlling the practice itself.

Digital fabrication played a critical role in this shift: laser cutters and 3D printers have successfully created new opportunities in design, in particular for a renewal of traditional printing methods, such as letterpress. 3D-printed or laser-cut typefaces are compelling examples of how these techniques can empower professional practice and the creative process. Over recent years, the organic implementation of digital fabrication serving traditional printing techniques has contributed to expand the community of designers around them and has empowered, through a return to craft, a reconsideration of the printed object in a post-digital era.

DIY, open-source, and hacker models have been proven relevant for empowering the graphic design practice and its creative process. By investigating auto-didactic and auto-productive practices within an educational institution, the project *Mobile Uno* is an invitation to capitalise on limitations, constraints, and imperfections, to prepare the next generation of designers to think critically about their practice, their tools, and new technological opportunities.

References

2017 CAST symposium being material: Ben Fry and Casey Reas, programmable (2017). https://www.youtube.com/watch?v=9BtqBjGEpA0.

Gachadoat, J. (2014). *Le Tricodeur*. V3ga. http://www.v3ga.net/blog2/2014/10/le-tricodeur/.

Google Design (2015). *Making material design*. https://www.youtube.com/watch?v=rrT6v5sOwJg.

Harrison, A. (2014) *A23D: A 3D-printed letterpress font, 2014*. https://vimeo.com/106092839.
He, L. (n.d.) *Licia He*. http://eyesofpanda.com/.
New North Press (2014). *A23D: A 3D-printed letterpress font*. New North Press. http://new-north-press.co.uk/project/a23d/.
Open Press Project (n.d.) *Our Story*. Open Press Project. https://openpressproject.com/pages/about-us.
Provisional Press (n.d.a) *Home*. Provisional Press. https://www.provisionalpress.com.
Provisional Press (n.d.b) *Laser cut plans*. Provisional Press. https://www.provisionalpress.com/laser-cut-plans.
p98a (2016) *Making our own type*. p98a. https://www.p98a.com/collection/making-our-own-type.
Triclot, M. (2011). *Philosophie Des Jeux Vidéo*. https://www.editions-zones.fr/lyber?philosophie-des-jeux-video#chapitre4.

10 Computational Design Letterpress

From Procedural Programming to Modular Printing

Pedro Amado and Ana Catarina Silva

Introduction

Today's designers and students have "almost unlimited freedom to define the forms, proportions, and widths of characters" (Blokland cit. by Hurka & Békés, 2019). New projects must consider different approaches since they are no longer bound by former technological constraints and have unprecedented access to history and openness to speculative design strategies (Dunne & Raby, 2013). However, despite the benefits of working digitally with computers in the graphic design or visual arts learning environment (Yeoh, 2002), due to the challenges that the global digital economy poses to education (Cezzar, 2020; Dziobczenski et al., 2018), design education is moving towards a heutagogical approach. But there is a general lack of investment in the research-led, design process, as well as hands-on experience of the production of tangible artefacts (Pontis & van der Waarde, 2020).

This chapter reflects on the intersection of computational design thinking, digital fabrication and manual printing. It discusses the result of harnessing the computational power of the parametric, algorithmic, or generative workflows through scripting procedures, for established design processes. In conjunction with an agile production process, this enables the emergence of innovative results out of initial abstraction (Menges & Ahlquist, 2011).

To assess the creative potential of this hybrid intersectional space, we have designed a three-stage experience, in which participants are introduced to the programming, design and digital fabrication of modular matrices for printing, using manual proof presses. Notwithstanding the controlled and mathematical quality of the first two stages, the expressive and combinatorial nature of the third stage—the letterpress-based printing stage—facilitates unexpected results. By controlling the tools and the process, free from standardised, centrally developed software (Mitchell, cit. by Terzidis, 2003), designers can iteratively navigate the previous stages, exploring

DOI: 10.4324/9781003173113-16

the creative potential and programmatically generated complexities of this hybrid process (Kolarevic, 2001).

Since the late 1980s, computational tools and techniques have been developed to aid print design and production. Described as "parametric," "algorithmic" or "generative design," these are only some of the approaches available to computational design,

> [as] one way of using computers during the design process as a medium to design better or different. It uses the computational and combinatorial power of a computer to generate schemes that can be useful to designers. It can also help designers synthesize forms, alter their shapes, and combine solids in ways often unpredictable.
>
> (Terzidis, 2015, p. 3)

In recent years, computational design has shifted current processes from making into finding forms (Agkathidis, 2016), thereby emphasising the "thinking" aspect of the process.

These approaches can be described by basing their approach on a set of rules, algorithms, or code supported by computational design tools—such as Processing—that enable a complex scripted design solution. The designer then shifts from being an operator to becoming the system's designer and conductor (Groß et al., 2018). Additionally, the output can be fed back into the process, informing the designer, who is then able to modify the rules or algorithm in a process of [post-]digital morphogenesis (Koralevic, 2009). Some designers and educators are still sceptical of unconventional approaches, but when used appropriately these inevitably support creativity and innovation (Agkathidis, 2016).

This chapter begins by presenting an overview of related projects and initiatives that employ hybrid approaches to digital design, analogue production and digital fabrication, within varied commercial production, hobbyist, hacking and educational practice contexts. Finally, we present the design and development of a computational design letterpress workshop as a case study application of methodology developed to contribute with computational design thinking to the current design education curricula.

Traditional, Digital and Hybrid Design Contexts

Font Design and Digital Fabrication

A23D[1] is an award-winning 3D-printed letterpress font commissioned by Richard Ardagh of New North Press and designed by Scott Williams and Henrik Kubel of A2-Type. Funded by the Arts Council, the goal of the

Computational Design Letterpress 115

project was to connect old and new technologies (Chalk Studios, 2014). This particular project takes advantage of the quality and resistance of what production-level polymer 3D printers have achieved (Walters, 2014). With almost no finishings necessary (as with wood type) this technology allows for a much more intricate and robust design, only possible in lead slugs, or zinc metal plates. Allowing complex and updated letterforms to be fabricated directly breathes new life into the design of shapes and finds new forms of expression.

The Revival of the Printed Poster

Dafi Kühne is a graphic designer and a self-taught letterpress printer. Driven by the desire to break the design limitations of interfering during the production stage, Kühne uses a comprehensive multi-stage production process that encompasses both digital and analogue techniques in two and three dimensions (Barmetter, in Caduff, 2016, p. 5). Although this is a very demanding process, from the designer's point of view, it enables the designer to refine, iterate and modify the work at any stage and add design value to client-based commercial projects (Shields, in Caduff, 2016, p. 12).

Digital Designs on Analogue Media

Jan-Villem van der Looij is an award-winning traditional letterpress printer that explores the expression of failed registration and printing errors (TDC, 2019). He runs his workshop—Mizdruk—where he produces, exhibits and sells his prints and publications. He welcomes partnerships and residencies with artists and designers, such as Melanie De Luca. As a result of such collaboration, he has developed the Letterpress Analogue Pixel Alphabet Project, with the type designer Pieter van Rosmalen from the Bold Monday type foundry. Rosmalen has designed a custom monospaced modular font—Pixel—that was materialised on photopolymer matrices and then used to print modular typographic compositions in several overprinted layers and interweaving the patterns.

Open-Source Presses

The Open Press project,[2] developed by Martin Schneider and Dominik Schmitz, consists of an accessible DIY 3D-printed small-format printmaking press that does not require specialty or heavy-duty printing plates. With the growing availability of consumer-grade 3D printers, and the ease of distributing the plans online for free, on websites such as Thingiverse,[3] this kind of project bridges the gap where previously designers and printers couldn't afford accessible printing equipment. Providing the plans and instructions in an open-source model also permits hacking and customisation by individuals and educational institutions.

Collaborative Workshop(s) and Modular Compositions

Richard Kegler (P22) and Jennifer Farrell (Starshaped Press) have revived a modular font design (Alpha-Blox from ATF) and fabricated it in plastic: the P22 Blox. These are available commercially but are primarily used in educational contexts. The lightweight and friendly nature of the material is more accessible to beginners. Its geometric-based modules are simple enough to be mastered in a few minutes and make it possible to produce complex and stimulating compositions. As in other similar initiatives, in conjunction with Amelia Hugill-Fontanel, they organise and promote workshops where they explore the surprising versatility and seemingly unlimited possibilities of printing with a modular system (Chandler, 2021).

Editorial Design and Self-Publishing Workshop(s)

Oficina do Cego[4] is a non-profit cultural association founded by a collective of artists and graphic designers whose aim is twofold: production of editorial objects and education of the general public. Whether through short workshops or long courses, participants are encouraged to experiment and use multiple technologies and media, combining them to produce hybrid post-digital artefacts, in a non-biased way.

Accessible Educational Printing Processes

The Provisional Press[5] is one of many resources made available by Steve Garst. He focuses on making letterpress type and printing accessible through non-traditional methods and relies on three core principles: usability, durability and ease of production. The project was created during the Covid-19 pandemic (released in July 2020) to provide an affordable and portable DIY press to students who were having a remote learning experience. It can work as a transitional press for people who do not have access to traditional steel presses and may generate thousands of prints if handled with care.

Computational Design Thinking Approaches

AlphaGraph[6] is a parametric customised tool developed in Processing by Mark Webster to explore letterforms. Based on a grid that displays points and lines, it allows the user to redesign a pre-existing font by handling a set of parameters (form, grid, colour, among others). The output is a vector graphic that can be used to create printing matrices, using digital fabrication methods. This tool has been used in an educational environment, with graphic design students, in several workshops and design courses, such as Parametric,[7] Lettrines[8,] or Lettres Ornées.[9] In these experiments, participants play with the possibilities of parametric drawing and the materiality of letterpress printing.

Computational Design Letterpress: A Case Study

As a warm-up activity for the Post-Digital Letterpress Printing international conference,[10] we have designed and organised an educational workshop that aims to bridge traditional printing practices with computational design. It combines the computational design thinking approach—such as algorithmic thinking, programmatic problem-solving and morphogenetic procedures—with the main steps of the letterpress process—context and constraints identification, form composition, colour separation, page imposition and proof press printing (Amado, Quelhas, Silva, 2019). This led to the event's name: "void pull() { return press(); } workshop. From procedural digital programming to modular letterpress printing"[11] in a functional approach.

Building on the ideas and methods from the aforementioned authors—in particular Rosmalen and de Looij's Analogue pixels, and Richard Kegler's P22 Blox—the practical goal of this workshop is to produce a short run of collective modular prints with participants.

Specifically, with procedural modular graphics generation through computer programming. The workshop is structured across three stages: (1) computational design; (2) digital fabrication; (3) analogue printing. The first edition of this workshop was held in an in-person mode. Although it may be possible to organise and host this workshop online[12] (e.g. using the Provisional or the Open Press kits), it is mainly intended to work in laboratories (fab labs) or DIY spaces that introduce participants to the process and allow them to be more independent.

The first stage—computational design—began its activities by providing foundational skills in computer programming using the Processing[13] environment. The first step is to address drawing functions and export graphics in a PDF vector format—the main advantage of using the java-based desktop version of Processing. The workshop programme then provides a brief foundation to transversal functional and object-oriented programming language concepts, such as variables, functions, loops and conditions. These concepts are the minimum viable set of skills that need to be addressed to produce a set of parametrically generated geometrical compositions. During the workshop, participants are also introduced to the work of visual artists and designers, in particular two Portuguese conceptual artists, Maria Keil and António Quadros Ferreira, whose work is based on modular or pattern-based algorithmic compositions (Amado & Martins, 2021).

After a brief session of bug correction and further coding assistance, the second phase focuses on transforming digital compositions into 3D-printed modules that are later used as typographical matrices to be imposed into a collective printing form. Depending on their proficiency and speed, they are encouraged to think and design their compositions in two separate layers or colours, using consumer-grade laser engravers and 3D UV resin printers, making the necessary prototyping adjustments.

We have found out that by using a consumer-grade SLA 3D printer with UV resin[14] it is possible to produce accurate, press resistant and reusable modules, suitable for a flatbed proof press or hand-operated platen presses. Given that it takes several minutes to produce type-high modules, we have opted to mimic traditional 3mm photopolymer plates and mount them on a base to obtain the type-high module on the press. This permits faster printer-to-imposition turnaround times, that are crucial to enable a fast-paced agile workflow: while some participants fabricate their modules, others test-print their compositions. During this stage, participants tweak or correct their designs, taking into account the colour combination, scale or interaction with other participants and their modular compositions in the imposition (Figure 10.1).

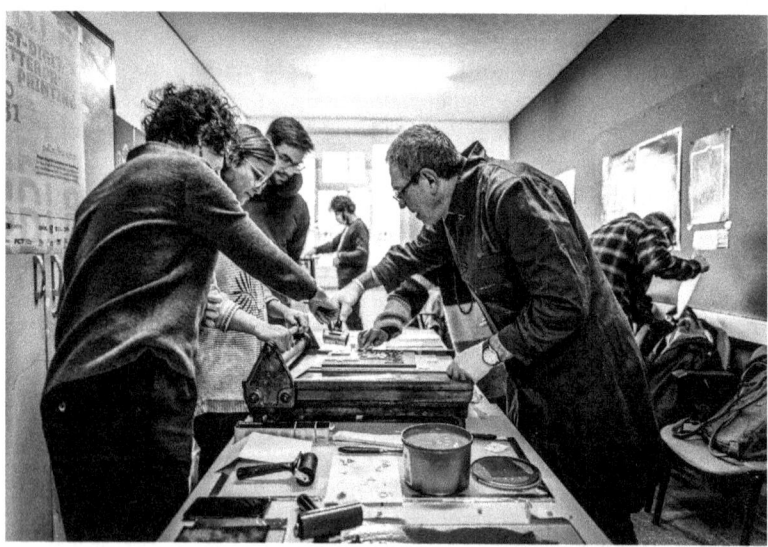

Figure 10.1 Participants Inking a Collaborative Mixed-Media Imposition on a Flatbed Proof Press, while Others are 3D Printing a Module.

The third and final phase concentrates on creating and printing a collaborative imposition. In this phase, participants experience colour mixing and test printing. Participants try out several impositions, combining the modules using one or two colours. This makes it possible to experience the overprint and material nature of the ink and press. By calibrating the height of the imposition, participants proceed with more heavily indented results or rough textures. And participants were able to obtain more intense or blurred layers by varying the quantity and thickness of the ink employed. Despite being able to reproduce some of these features in the computer, participants can comprehend them better and faster by experiencing them physically.

Conclusion

The process of designing the algorithms to describe and set tiling pattern compositions shares the same modular nature as the letterpress process. Although Computational Design is not limited by any specific factor, as with letterpress, its constraints reflect the available material and hardware that will be employed in subsequent fabrication. As such, design constraints are important and present in both contexts: in letterpress, the limitations are linked to the available material for composition; in computational design, the limitations are intrinsic to the knowledge and experience of the designer. While the former stimulates the creative problem-solving approach, the latter promotes generative expression in the design phase (Sawyer, 2012).

The modular nature of letterpress is the foundation for many design and typography concepts, essential for graphic designers and visual artists. While the physical nature of letterpress enforces a strict composition ruleset—as modules cannot overlap one another in the same imposition—participants must design or develop a sense of composition using modularity and hierarchy, especially taking the negative space into account in their designs. Computational design makes it possible to create almost infinite and flexible rules and design combinations. Yet, using a procedural approach reinforces the modularity nature of the algorithms present in the final composition. And by being able to procedurally explore the compositions in code (by design, or by trial-and-error) participants can visualise new possibilities with unprecedented speed, ease, complexity and emergent possibilities (Gross et al., 2018; Sawyer, 2012).

This does not mean that the compositions are defined by the computer algorithm—in a sense of Artificial Creativity—but it is expected that this process will stimulate the three main types of creativity: combinational; exploratory; and transformational (Boden, 2016).

By being able to iterate back and forth between design, fabrication and composition, we believe that computational design letterpress may provide better and more comprehensive computational design thinking foundations, enhance the capability to design within constraints, develop the compositional skills of participants and finally provide some insight into historical and technical print production processes by achieving control and intervention in all stages of the design and production process.

This experimental approach is relevant more than ever to the current post-digital computational design practices. As computers, digital design and fabrication tools become ubiquitous, users require an ever-expanding skillset to use them in an autonomous, creative and responsible way. As consumer-grade digital fabrication equipment provides faster, cheaper and more accurate results, it is possible to envision a near future, where these tools will be available to everyone. It is also relevant to take into account the current and future challenges to in-person and online-based activities for remote teaching, design and production. Having such equipment in people's homes and offices—not needing to send files for remote or local production—accelerates the design iteration process, allowing for a more agile and insightful exploration of the results, returning materiality and craftsmanship to design.

Notes

1. http://new-north-press.co.uk/project/a23d/.
2. https://openpressproject.com/.
3. As they did in 2018, by publishing the files that facilitated printing an Open Press at home: https://www.thingiverse.com/thing:2841592.
4. http://oficinadocego.blogspot.com/.
5. https://www.provisionalpress.com/.
6. https://bitbucket.org/mwebster_/alphagraph/src/master/.
7. https://parametrictype.bitbucket.io/.
8. http://workshop-lettrine-01.esad-amiens.fr/.
9. https://www.flickr.com/photos/tisane_01/32104109192/in/album-72157626131513583/.
10. https://pdlp.fba.up.pt/.
11. Description, programme, and results available online at: https://pdlp.fba.up.pt/warm-up-workshops.html#vprp.
12. We conducted the first digital part of this workshop in a strictly online mode in 2021, during the Processing Community Day conference (https://pcd.fba.up.pt/2021/#workshops). Some educators, such A.B. Gorham, Director of the Black Rock Press of the University of Nevada, used DIY printing kits with some degree of success in online contexts (Morimoto, 2020).
13. Processing is a computer programming environment that encompasses a Java-based simplified language and IDE, especially developed for Graphic Designers and Visual Artists at MIT available for Macintosh, Windows and Linux operating systems.
14. We've employed an AnyCubic Photon model with UV Resin washable with isopropyl alcohol. Since then, water washable UV resins have become widely available and, despite being slightly more expensive, are easier and safer to employ.

References

Agkathidis, A. (2016). *Generative design: Form-finding techniques in architecture*. Lawrence King Publishing Ltd.

Amado, P., & Martins, N. (2021). Procedural pattern interpretations of the work of António Quadros Ferreira. In *Threads of a legacy: Towards a pedagogical heritage in art and design: The Porto school of fine arts, 1956–1984* (pp 115–125). Porto: FBAUP/ID+. ISBN 978-989-33-1203-2.

Amado, P., Quelhas, V., & Silva, A. C. (2019). Revival of letterpress: The Portuguese scenario. In Tavares, P. (Org.) (2019). *CAOS communication, art and object synergies – Practice research, the time is now. DRX: Registos de Investigação em Design* (pp 81–97). Aveiro: Universidade de Aveiro. ISBN 978-989-99861-9-0.

Boden, M. A. (2016). *AI: Its nature and future*. New York: Oxford University Press.

Caduff, R. (Ed.) (2016). *True print*. Zurich: Lars Müller Publishers.

Cezzar, J. (2020). Teaching the designer of now: A new basis for graphic and communication design education. *She Ji*, 6(2), 213–227. https://doi.org/10.1016/j.sheji.2020.05.002

Chandler, C. (2021). *Long-distance letterpress: Modular typography*. Partners in Print. https://partnersinprint.org/event/long-distance-letterpress-modular-typography-2/

Dunne, A., & Raby, F. (2013). *Speculative everything: Design, fiction, and social dreaming*. Cambridge, MA: MIT Press.

Dziobczenski, P. R. N., Person, O., & Meriläinen, S. (2018). Designing career paths in graphic design: A document analysis of job advertisements for graphic design positions in Finland. *The Design Journal*, 21(3), 349–370. https://doi.org/10.1080/14606925.2018.1444874

Groß, B., Bohnacker, H., Laub, J., & Lazzeroni, C. (2018). *Generative design: visualize, program, and create with JavaScript in p5.js*. New York: Princeton Architectural Press.

Hurka, C., & Békés, N. (2019). *Reviving type: Practice based research on Renaissance and Baroque models compared and discussed*. Rotterdam: Acute Publisher.

Kolarevic, B. (2001). Designing and manufacturing architecture in the digital age. *CumInCAD*. http://papers.cumincad.org/cgi-bin/works/paper/3826

Kolarevic, B. (2009). *Architecture in the digital age: Design and manufacturing*. New York: Spon Press.

Menges, A., & Ahlquist, S. (2011). *Computational design thinking: Computation design thinking*. Chichester: Chichester: John Wiley & Sons.

Morimoto, T. (2020). *School of the Arts professors persevere to educate and inspire students*. Reno, NV: University of Nevada, Reno. Nevada Today. https://www.unr.edu/nevada-today/news/2020/school-of-the-arts-professors-teach-students-during-pandemic

Pontis, S., & van der Waarde, K. (2020). Looking for alternatives: Challenging assumptions in design education. *She Ji*, 6(2), 228–253. https://doi.org/10.1016/j.sheji.2020.05.005

Sawyer, R. K. (2012). *Explaining creativity – The science of human innovation* (2nd ed.). New York: Oxford University Press.

Studios, C. (2014). *A23D A 3D printed letterpress typeface*. Chalk Studios. http://www.chalkstudios.co.uk/project/a23d-3d-printed-letterpress/

TDC. (2019). *Mizdruk*. Type Directors Club. https://www.tdc.org/work/mizdruk/

Terzidis, K. (2003). *Expressive form: A conceptual approach to computational design*. New York: Spon Press.

Terzidis, K. (2015). *Permutation design: Buildings, texts, and contexts*. Oxon; New York: Routledge.

Walters, J. L. (2014). *AK and A23D on press*. Eye Magazine. http://www.eyemagazine.com/blog/post/AK-and-A23D-on-press

Yeoh, K. C. (2002). *A study on the influences of computer usage on idea formation in graphic design students*. Lubbock: Univ. of Texas.

Conclusion

Pedro Amado, Ana Catarina Silva and Vítor Quelhas

Letterpress can be defined as the process of using movable characters—different types of letters, marks, and symbols, usually made of wood and metal—to set and print compositions on assorted physical media. The definitions are varied, but most seem to converge on a step-based process: knowing the client and the purpose of the job; understanding the context, the material available for printing, and the restrictions or limitations for the job; conceptualising the idea; composing; proofing; pagination; imposition and furniture handling; printing; unimposing and distributing the case; and the finishings. Of these, the composition, imposition, and printing are the most important steps that are usually mentioned. But, especially in the current digitally connected world, additional stages, such as physical and digital distribution or promotion, are also extremely important, although not exclusive of the letterpress printing process.

Today letterpress encompasses much more: as a process, it is useful to understand and expand the notion of physical and digital compositions as modular systems of rules.

Due to the blurring of the boundaries between printing, design, and art, letterpress is no longer a medium of a specific field of study and allows us to merge different fields. Digital fabrication empowers more users to explore this field creatively as the physical or commercial barriers that letterpress traditionally imposes are lowered. It is possible to cast specific sizes, formats, or materials of sorts, which are explored in innovative and creative ways. Designers and printers now search not only for a "clean" print but also for experimental and expressive compositions, often involving multidisciplinary collaborations. The possibility of exploring an alternative and slower material process of design is alluring for younger generations who have been brought up on immaterial interactions. The experience of the process is almost as important—if not more—than the result, the artifacts themselves. So much that, practitioners not only record the entire process

DOI: 10.4324/9781003173113-102

of creating these artefacts in an audiovisual format but also often add value through storytelling in the dissemination of the process on social media.

Whether to conduct research or to push the materiality, expression, and production methods, educational institutions try to preserve this technology and practice by maintaining or adding it to their curricula. Not only to provide added value to projects, but also as a comprehensive way to teach students the foundations of digital design and the printing process. The letterpress process, as a whole, makes it possible to explore specific material phases, such as preparing the plates, colour tuning, imposition, and especially the final printing of the work. It remains an exclusive medium that provides access to the print-production process usually hidden behind digital hardware or software. Most importantly it is a physical way to learn and to teach the history and technical aspects of typography, in a holistic and comprehensive way.

The main challenge for letterpress today continues to be its commercial viability—it is no longer viable to do it the traditional way. At the same time, it presents an opportunity to find new and interesting ways to use it and combine it with other technologies, to pursue artistic collaborations, or to explore innovative commercial endeavours.

We hope this book has presented you with a comprehensive and current view of this field. Whether you are a researcher, seasoned professional, or an art and design student, we have aimed to make this book both inclusive and useful. More than a historical record, we expect this book to provide the roadmap for upcoming generations of artists, designers, printers, and makers to make the most of future challenges.

Index

3D: -printed type 6, 7; -printed typeface 106; printers 97; printing 65, 69, 108, 118

A2-Type 108, 114
A23D 65, 73, 106, 108
AHP Six 106
Aitkin, John 14
alphabets: lead 76; wood 76
Alpha-Blox 118
American Type Founders 3, 4, 116
Analogue Pixel Alphabet Project 115
Architectural Types 108
Ardagh, Richard 71, 108, 114; see also A23D; New North Press
Atêlie Acaia 43

Bauersche Giesserei 58
Bold Monday type foundry 115
Brown, John 11
Bruce Jr., David 96, 101
Burrill, Anthony 65

cabinets: furniture 51; type 52
casting 4, 96
catalogues: font 49; type 53
Caxton, William 9
Charny, Daniel 42
Cimatti, Federico 43
Cloister: Initials 1, 4–6
CNC 35, 69, 95, 97, 98, 100, 101, 106
craft: based local economy xxi; -based trade 12; making 43
craftsmanship 96, 97, 102, 120
Crown Albion Press 12
Culefant, John 13

Digilog Prints 70
DIY 101, 105–108, 110, 111, 115–117
Duke of Cumberland 11

Eveillard, Louis 106

Farrell, Jennifer 116
Fausto Galico Fonderia 58
FDM 6
Fior, Robin 42–43, 78–80
Fisher, Herbert 32
Fonderie Typographique Française 58
Forme 70
Fregio Gloria 58
Froshaug, Anthony 41
Fry, Ben 104, 107
Fundición José Iranzo 57, 58; see also José Iranzo Foundry
Fundición Tipográfica Nacional 21, 58
Futura Schmuck 58

galley sheet 51–53
Garst, Liz 107; see also Garst, Steve; Provisional Press
Garst, Steve 96, 100–102, 107, 116
Giant Pivotal caster 4
Gil, José 79
Goudy, Frederic W. 3, 4, 6
Goudy Initials 4; see also Cloister
Goudy: Initials, no. 296 4; *Old Style* 3

Hamilton Manufacturing Company 99
Hamilton Wood Type & Printing Museum 65, 99
Hatch Show Print, 98, 101

Heidelberg: cylinder press 21; platen presses 21
Hogarth Press 12, 32–35; see also Woolf, Virginia; Woolf, Leonard
Homem do Saco 79

Imprensa Nacional 49

Jeffery, Desmond 43
Johnson, John 10
José Iranzo Foundry 57; see also Fundición José Iranzo

Kegler, Richard 4, 116, 117; see also Alpha-Blox; P22; P22, Blox
Kennedy, Amos Paul 65
Kindel, Eric 41
Kitching, Alan 79
Kubel, Henrik 108, 114
Kühne, Dafi 65, 115

Lanston Monotype 4; see also Monotype
laser: cut 61, 63, 98, 106, 109–111; cutter 98–101, 107; cutting 61, 69, 95, 99, 101, 106; engraved 5, 6, 65; engraving 6, 69
L'Automàtica 43
Leavenworth, William 96
Lee Priory Press 10
Lettergieterij 21
letterpress: aesthetic 98, 101; aesthetics of xix; business 43; communities 43; printing 1, 12, 19, 27, 28, 60, 65, 76, 78, 79, 81, 86, 95, 96, 100, 102, 106, 117, 123; process 95, 117, 119, 124; technology xviii, 61, 71; workers xxi, 68; workshop 19, 21, 32, 39, 40, 75, 76, 81, 106, 109, 114
Linotype 49
Litografia Minho 20
Litografia Pátria 20
Looij, Jan-Villem van der 115; see also Mizdruk
Lowthorp, John 13

Madame de Pompadour 11
maker: -cultures 39, 42; movements 97; -networks 43
Mallarmé, Stéphane xviii, 89

master craftsman 47
matrices 4–5, 69, 96, 114–118
Mayo, Thomas 65, 106
McKellier Woodtype 99
mechanical typesetting 12
Merelau-Ponty, Maurice 33
Mizdruk 115
modular: compositions 116, 118; elements 69; font 115, 116; kit 104, 106; logic 58; printing 117; standardization 61; system 39, 56, 58, 60, 61; typeface 62
Molloy, Ryan 96, 100, 106
Monotype 5, 12, 49
Moore, Scott 96, 99–102, 107
Moore Wood Type 99, 107; see also Moore, Scott

Nesbitt Roman Grotesque 100
New North Press 65, 106, 108, 114; see also Ardagh, Richard
Norb Brylski 99
NOVADAM 58

offset lithography 12–15
Oficina do Cego 116
Open Press Project 107–108, 115

P22 4–6, 116–117; Blox 116; see also Alpha-Blox; American Type Founders
p98a 65, 106
pantograph 49, 96, 100, 106; cutting 99
Paulo de Cantos 77
Petrescu Press 99
photopolymer 5, 35, 69, 107, 115, 118; see also plates
pivotal typecaster 4, 96
plates: 3D-printed 5; analogue letterpress 5; birch veneer plywood 98; engraved xix; magnesium 6; photopolymer 6, 35, 107, 118; zinc 5, 115; zinc engraving 21, 27
Poisson, Jeanne Antoinette 11; see also Madame de Pompadour
post-digital: age 66; letterpress 68–71; period 6
Prensa La Libertad 43
printer: master 9; pirate- 13–15
printing trade 9, 12, 97, 101

private presses 10
processes: analogue 105; creative 66–67, 108; digital 5, 54, 82, 105; formative 97; hybrid 85; joining 97; manufacturing 96; planographic 100; printing 48, 116; standardized 5; subtractive manufacturing 95, 97; unorthodox 105
Provisional Press 100–101, 107–108; see also Garst, Liz; Garst, Steve

Reas, Casey 104, 107
Richards, Vyvyan 12
RISO 76, 105–106
risograph 75, 78, 83; see also RISO
Roach, James 14; see also Roach, John
Roach, John 14
Rosmalen, Pieter van 115
rubber stamps 62

Schmitz, Dominik 107, 115
Schneider, Martin 107, 115
Shaw, Frederic 14
Starshaped Press 116; see also Farrell, Jennifer
Stempel AG 58
stencil 61, stencils 39, 101
Stereolithographic 3D printing: printer 118; process 6
Super Tipo Veloz 57–64
Sutter, John 11

Ticoolgrafia 77
Toorn, Jan van 44

Trochut, Àlex 58; see also Trochut, Joan; Trochut, Ettienne
Trochut, Ettienne 58; see also Trochut, Joan; Trochut, Àlex
Trochut, Joan 57, 58; see also Trochut, Ettienne; Trochut, Àlex
type: composed 31; composer 35, 92; case 51–53; design 56–63; digital 5, 63, 98; dissed 31; lack of 81–83; metal 4–6, 63, 70, 78, 95–98; movable 47–54, 63, 69–70, 87–91; system 61; wood 52, 65, 76, 95–101, 115
typecaster 4, 96
typeface design 1, 3
typesetting 12, 30–31, 37, 60–61, 70, 98, 106

Vandercook 5, 43
Vetter, Brad 96, 98, 102
Virgin Wood Type Manufacturing Company 99

Walters, Gregory 4
Warwick, John 10
Webster, Mark 116
Wells, Darius 96
Wilkes, John 10
Williams, Scott 108, 114; see also Kubel, Henrik; A2-Type
woodcuts 32, 98
Woolf, Leonard 32; see also Woolf, Virginia; Hogarth Press
Woolf, Virginia 12–13, 30–38; see also Woolf, Leonard; Hogarth Press
Wright, Edward 41

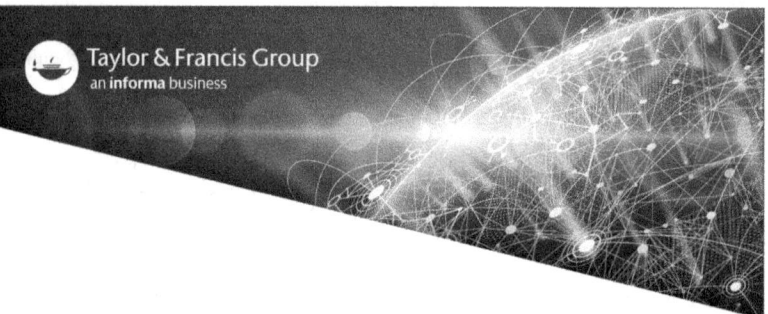

Taylor & Francis eBooks

www.taylorfrancis.com

A single destination for eBooks from Taylor & Francis with increased functionality and an improved user experience to meet the needs of our customers.

90,000+ eBooks of award-winning academic content in Humanities, Social Science, Science, Technology, Engineering, and Medical written by a global network of editors and authors.

TAYLOR & FRANCIS EBOOKS OFFERS:

- A streamlined experience for our library customers
- A single point of discovery for all of our eBook content
- Improved search and discovery of content at both book and chapter level

REQUEST A FREE TRIAL
support@taylorfrancis.com

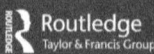 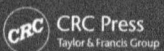

For Product Safety Concerns and Information please contact our EU
representative GPSR@taylorandfrancis.com
Taylor & Francis Verlag GmbH, Kaufingerstraße 24, 80331 München, Germany

www.ingramcontent.com/pod-product-compliance
Lightning Source LLC
Chambersburg PA
CBHW051750230426
43670CB00012B/2226